How Precious the Ground on Which We Stand

for,

With best wishes,

Kelly Luna

Sheldon Lewis

How Precious the Ground on Which We Stand

Jewish Values that Could Save the Earth

Hakodesh Press

Publisher:
Hakodesh Press
is a trademark of
Dodo Books Indian Ocean Ltd. and OmniScriptum S.R.L publishing group

120 High Road, East Finchley, London, N2 9ED, United Kingdom
Str. Armeneasca 28/1, office 1, Chisinau MD-2012, Republic of Moldova, Europe
Printed at: see last page
ISBN: 978-620-2-45530-5

For my grandchildren, for all grandchildren,
and the grandchildren of every species who depend on a vital Earth
on which to grow, to play, and to thrive.

Contents

Preface

I have never felt this way before. There have always been urgent needs to meet in our very imperfect and often unjust world. Gun violence, refugees, terrorism, outbreaks of war, undisguised racism, bigotry, growing inequality, and so much more clamor for our attention every day. Yet, I do not recall in my lifetime or in the lifetime of our forebears a crisis bearing down on us so quickly that threatens the viability of all people and all species on the very ground on which we stand. As I write these words, unprecedented wildfires flare uncontrolled around the world while in other places, flooding endangers everyone in its path as the Earth unnaturally warms. It feels as though there is little if any time to spare. No one is unaffected. Actions surely have been undertaken; many are very ambitious. Yet it feels as though as planetary citizens **we have not come close to the full awakening we need to change our current trajectory towards an uninhabitable world caused by climate change brought about by human hands.**

I confess I have been slow to reach awareness and to act. Finally, I decided to ask myself, how can I change even though I am not an expert on climate, nor do I hold a position of power? I am acting out of a belief that I learned from my beloved teacher Abraham Joshua Heschel who taught frequently and passionately: "Some are guilty, but all are responsible." As inhabitants of planet Earth, we have witnessed, benefitted from, and contributed to the abuse of our only home in the cosmos. Now there is urgency for everyone to act in accordance with the gifts we have been given. Because I am a rabbi, I turn to the treasury of wisdom embodied in Jewish tradition searching for motivation and guidance.

For almost three years in my congregation in California, a group of volunteers have worked devotedly to raise the visibility of climate action among our members and to seek meaningful ways to contribute. Calling ourselves "L'olam Va-ed", a play on a familiar Hebrew phrase meaning "forever", we recast these words as a prayer that the "olam", our world, never

5

end. While preparing for our lively bi-weekly meetings, I was often invited to ground our deliberations in Jewish values by sharing some words of Torah. I relished the assignment. I was surprised to find how easy it was to locate climate wisdom in Torah! I had only to check the passages where human life and the Earth intersect along with accompanying rabbinic commentary. My quest for Div're Torah was so rewarding and almost effortless. I was often overcome by powerful ideas hiding in plain sight which I could not wait to share with our L'olam Va-ed steering team.

We are taught mysteriously that Torah has 70 faces. This is simply another way of claiming that Torah has unlimited treasuries of wisdom awaiting to be unlocked. In my privileged upbringing where I was introduced to the vast library of sacred texts and rabbinic interpretation, I learned that there was no end of ways to understand each verse and even each word. Yet, I overlooked a key reason why there remains this ever present, ever fruitful, ever evolving possibility for uncovering a new face of Torah. When Torah is read through the lens of a pressing issue, in a context which perhaps has never been encountered, Torah can speak in a fresh voice. We finally have eyes to see and an open heart to hear.

The climate crisis insists itself upon us more urgently each day. I have been a student of Torah for so much of my life, but I am still totally stunned by what I have found regarding our relationship to this earth. I stand in awe at age-old ideas that teach a compelling new way of understanding our responsibilities vis a vis the Earth on which we stand. I now see texts and practices that have been woven into my life for decades but which I now understand in a new light. I am eager to invite you along on this old/new journey through Torah. I now see much more clearly a reservoir of hope for change, a reminder of our power as human beings, our need to be humble even while holding our power, our deep interconnectivity to the Earth and to all its creatures, and the dramatic reminders that the Earth does not belong to us. My heartfelt hope is that this view of Torah will lead to action. Urgency does not quite capture the precariousness of this moment for planet Earth.

Introduction

The Uniqueness of Climate Change as a Moral Challenge

The crisis brought on by climate change is qualitatively different from other very pressing concerns. Racism, inequality, gun control, civil discourse, and peacemaking among others call out desperately for our attention. Yet not one of those issues stands one whit of a chance for amelioration without a stable, sustainable Earth on which to wage our campaigns. Our planet provides the essential stage for doing acts of "Tikkun Olam", for "perfecting this world", for reaching for a better life for all.

The rabbis named what they thought was the bedrock upon which every desirable goal could be built:

אין כלי מחזיק ברכה אלא השלום

There is no vessel that can contain blessing other than peace.[1]

From their perspective and experience, the rabbis were convinced that if peace were not achievable, any other quest to accomplish something good for human life or for all of life would be elusive. Peace was the sine qua non for building every other blessing. With violent conflict as a backdrop, how could one hope to work successfully for any other worthy goal? In the hierarchy of values, peace was the hard rock upon which every other value depended.

These noble sages did not face a world of record and lethal heat, of rising seas, of constantly more destructive storms, of pollution on a grand scale caused by human activity. If they had, they might have reframed their conclusion about a baseline for thriving today:

אין כלי מחזיק ברכה אלא כדור הארץ בר קימא

There is no vessel that can contain blessing other than a sustainable Earth.

---

1 Bamidbar Rabba, 21:1

If we awaken each day to an increasingly endangered and wounded planet, every wish we might harbor would be fruitless. There would be more scarcity, more insecurity, more uncertainty about tomorrow. Without a stable, healthy platform on which to act, we would regress into the horrors of dystopia. All our dreams are built upon a friendly, magnificent planet where we can work to perfect our shared future together.

There is more that is unique about climate change. It is an issue that affects everyone without exception. Indeed, it is of great moment to every living species. Self-interest and altruism towards others are joined. When we commit to act, we are safeguarding ourselves and those that are dear to us; and we are reaching out to every stranger and every other species of plant and animal and to the Earth itself. Working on climate proclaims our global interdependence with a kind of clarity we have never known. To move the needle on this crisis, every country and its citizens must be committed. From the grass roots to the highest levels of government, everyone is summoned to action. We are completely dependent on one another to act with responsibility toward the whole. A parable of Rabbi Shimon bar Yochai makes this point:

תָּנֵי רַבִּי שִׁמְעוֹן בֶּן יוֹחָאי, מָשָׁל לִבְנֵי אָדָם שֶׁהָיוּ יוֹשְׁבִין בִּסְפִינָה נָטַל אֶחָד מֵהֶן מַקְדֵּחַ וְהִתְחִיל קוֹדֵחַ תַּחְתָּיו, אָמְרוּ לוֹ חֲבֵרָיו מַה אַתָּה יוֹשֵׁב וְעוֹשֶׂה, אָמַר לָהֶם מָה אִכְפַּת לָכֶם לֹא תַחְתִּי אֲנִי קוֹדֵם, אָמְרוּ לוֹ שֶׁהַמַּיִם עוֹלִין וּמְצִיפִין עָלֵינוּ אֶת הַסְּפִינָה

Rabbi Shimon bar Yochai taught a parable: People were on a ship. One of them took a drill and started drilling underneath him.

The others said to him: "What are you sitting there doing?!"

He replied: "What do you care? Is this not underneath my area that I am drilling?!"

They said to him: "But the water will rise and flood us all on this ship."[2]

---

2 Vayikra Rabbah 4:6

The actions of every individual can affect so many others. Yet, along the way in this struggle, there are very uneven effects. The developed nations that have spewed most of the heat-trapping gases into our atmosphere bear more responsibility for the record heat and intense storms that know no borders. The less privileged suffer unduly and are less able to adapt to this new reality. Inequality persists in this global crisis, and it must be addressed. Thus, climate justice is bound inextricably with climate action.

I AND THOU

One hundred years ago, Martin Buber published his seminal work **I And Thou.** As a teenager, I was very moved by his basic teaching that "all authentic living is meeting."[3] Back then, I learned his vocabulary to think and speak about our most basic need to thrive: to be in deep, honest, caring, fully present relationships with others. To be in an I-Thou relationship means that we are deeply committed to another, that we attempt to confirm each other's uniqueness, that we are curious about the other, ready to listen deeply, wanting to learn from others and to invest in relationships in depth.

Buber applied his teaching to the interhuman, between ourselves and others we meet; but he also testifies that one can experience such encounters with members of the animal and plant kingdoms. He tells of his own moving engagements with a horse[4] and a tree[5]. These accounts are mysterious, bordering on the mystical. Of course, the nature of such meetings must vary, and the reciprocity implicit in I-Thou must be other than a person-to-person encounter. Yet he insists that we can walk in the world seeking such unforgettable meetings. I cannot help thinking that Buber would apply his thinking even to the inanimate parts of the world, to the land, to water, and even to the air, to that which is indispensable for any life. What Buber has

---

3 Buber, Martin, I And Thou, (New York: Charles Scribner's Sons, 1958), p.11
4 Buber, Martin, Meetings, (LaSalle,Illinois: Open Court Publishing Company,1973), P. 26
5 Op Cit, Buber, Martin, I And Thou, p. 7

taught me is that we can live our lives in quest of meetings in depth with the world in all its manifestations.

Buber reminds us with his stirring insight that we should not take for granted all that inhabits the world around us. Face to face we can seek deeper relationships. To risk losing that possibility is unthinkable. To avoid losing what we love, we must care for this Earth and all that is in it.

We begin our journey through Torah. There is a chapter for each of the five books of the Chumash. Each one speaks urgently about our relationship to our world. Each of the following passages calls to us to act.

CHAPTER ONE

GENESIS

Recreating the World

The opening sentence in **Genesis** is surprising.

בְּרֵאשִׁית בָּרָא אֱלֹהִים אֵת הַשָּׁמַיִם וְאֵת הָאָרֶץ:

In the beginning, God created the heavens and the earth.[6]

Instead of using an unambiguous Hebrew word meaning "in the beginning" as many translations have it, the first Hebrew word בראשית is suggestive of varying interpretations. A Chassidic rendering understands the text to say that creation was imbued with the possibility of new beginnings. One could read the verse this way:

God created the heavens and the earth with "beginning".

or

God created the heavens and the earth with ever present potential for renewal.

It was not a one-time event. Inherently there was the capacity for a new start. How these new beginnings would be possible is indeterminate, and the text leaves out by whose agency the heavens and the earth could be re-created. Yet, the Torah begins with assurance that creativity is built into the very fabric of this world.

Jewish thought is founded on hope. In every age, there is a distance between the world as it is and the possibility for what it might still become. Repairing and perfecting the world (Tikkun Olam) became not only a theological axiom but a popular slogan as well. While faith in God's presence and power is affirmed, the power to renew is vested in human hands:

---

6 Genesis, 1:1

לְתַקֵּן עוֹלָם בְּמַלְכוּת שַׁדַּי

to perfect the world (in the image of) the kingdom of God.[7]

Usually, the arena of change is manageable, involving one's own life, one's community, or even one's nation. The challenge with climate change is that re-creation, tikkun olam, means repairing the entire Earth. Torah's first word implies that nothing is impossible, that a reset can come to be.

Radical Amazement

The story of creation is a powerful expression of wonder at the earth's richness. From nothingness comes an awesome unfolding of the world that we know and love. Astronomical wonders fall into place. The earth is separated from the heavens. The sun and the moon assume their roles above us while, on earth, bodies of water are contained, and dry land emerges. Plant life burgeons forth with each species bearing the ability to reproduce itself. The animal kingdom follows with enormous adaptations to thrive in the sea, to fly above, and to fill every niche on land. Each species is endowed with the ability and the mandate to reproduce itself. In fact, the animal kingdom is given the first commandment: פרו ורבו "Be fruitful and multiply"[8]. This outburst of life is exuberant and abundant.

Finally, the most complex of creatures, human beings, emerge, the most gifted of this outpouring of creativity. Once again, the commandment is reiterated: פרו ורבו ומלאו את הארץ "Be fruitful and multiply and fill the land."[9] Sustainability for growth over generations for all species of plants and animals is emphasized from the very beginning. Chapter 1 of Genesis cannot be read as science. Instead, it should be read as a simple, heartfelt outpouring of wonder at the world that is experienced by human observers.

Biblical writers could not yet imagine the richness still to be uncovered

---

7 Daily Liturgy within the "Oleynu" prayer culminating every service.
8 Genesis, 1:22
9 Genesis, 1:28

as human knowledge progressed. The microscope of Leeuwenhoek and the telescope of Galileo would display the unimaginable worlds beneath and above our normal range of vision. The Hubbell and Webb space telescopes have expanded our power to see light years away. Sources of wonder abound.

Abraham Joshua Heschel expressed deep concern about the weakening of our sense of wonder. He coined the expression "radical amazement." Here are his words:

As civilization advances, the sense of wonder declines. Such decline is an alarming symptom of our state of mind. Mankind will not perish for want of information; but only for want of appreciation. The beginning of our happiness lies in the understanding that life without wonder is not worth living. What we lack is not a will to believe but a will to wonder.

Awareness of the divine begins with wonder. It is the result of what man does with his higher incomprehension. The greatest hindrance to such awareness is our adjustment to conventional notions, to mental cliches. Wonder or radical amazement, the state of maladjustment to words and notions, is therefore a prerequisite for an authentic awareness of that which is.

Radical amazement has a wider scope than any other act of man. While any act of perception or cognition has as its object a selected segment of reality, radical amazement refers to all of reality; not only to what we see, but also to the very act of seeing as well as to our own selves, to the selves that see and are amazed at their ability to see.[10]

Heschel emphasized that our inability to sustain wonder at our world would have awful consequences, even causing the world to "perish".

The rabbinic tradition took on an urgent mission to keep wonder alive each day. In Jewish liturgy, the "ברכה" the "blessing", became one of the

---

10 Heschel, Abraham Joshua, God in Search of Man, (Philadelphia & New York: Jewish Publication Society and Meridian Books, 1961), p. 46

rabbis' greatest contributions. The simple formulation "Blessed are You", followed by specifying one of countless occasions for thanksgiving and for wonder, accompanies a Jew from awakening to going to bed at night. Every act of eating or drinking, sights, sounds, and fragrances, even normal bodily functions are occasions for a blessing. One aspires to say at least one hundred blessings each day with the goal to sharpen one's awareness of daily miracles and to nurture feelings of wonder and thanksgiving. One hundred blessings a day battles against taking the magnificence of the world for granted!

In Heschel's view, a vital sense of wonder is a prerequisite for taking action to hold onto the treasures that our eyes and hearts behold. If we manage to experience radical amazement each day, we will be motivated to act to preserve the sources of such wonder. A person with a vital sense of awe for this world is unlikely to despoil the Earth. Even more, that person would be moved to heal this wounded planet. Action is directly proportional to a sense of appreciation.

Springing From the Earth

On the sixth day of creation, the decision to create Adam was framed in a very unusual way:

וַיֹּאמֶר אֱלֹהִים נַעֲשֶׂה אָדָם בְּצַלְמֵנוּ כִּדְמוּתֵנוּ ·

And God said, "Let us make humankind in our image, after our likeness".[11]
Unlike all other acts of creation heretofore, the grammar changes from singular to plural with God seeming to invite another to share in this dramatic step. Who exactly is the other?

One suggestion attributed to Rabbi Moshe Kimche by the esteemed thinker and Biblical commentator Rabbi Moshe ben Nachman (known as

---

11 Genesis, 1:26

Ramban, 1194–1270) is that the partner God is addressing is the earth itself![12] The plant and animal kingdoms have sprung from the earth. They have been given their material form by the earth. Similarly, the soil is asked to generate Adam's physical form. The spiritual component will be the Divine gift. In the second chapter's more nuanced description of human creation:

וַיִּיצֶר יְהֹוָה אֱלֹהִים אֶת־הָאָדָם עָפָר מִן־הָאֲדָמָה וַיִּפַּח בְּאַפָּיו נִשְׁמַת חַיִּים וַיְהִי הָאָדָם לְנֶפֶשׁ חַיָּה:

God formed the human from the dust of the earth, blowing into his nostrils the breath of life: the human became a living being.[13]

Here the intimate bond between the human being and the soil is explicitly spelled out. The very existence of human beings on this planet is interwoven with the surface on which they stand.

Exercising Power

Empowering the first human beings, God's voice declares:

פְּרוּ וּרְבוּ וּמִלְאוּ אֶת־הָאָרֶץ וְכִבְשֻׁהָ וּרְדוּ בִּדְגַת הַיָּם וּבְעוֹף הַשָּׁמַיִם וּבְכָל־חַיָּה הָרֹמֶשֶׂת עַל־הָאָרֶץ:

Increase and multiply and fill the earth and master it; and rule the fish of the sea, the birds of the sky, and all the living things that creep on earth.[14]

From its earliest moments, humanity exercised power over the earth and its creatures. Unlike other species at least in degree, a human being could shape its environment either for good or for evil. The words describing human ability in this passage are strong: "וכבשוה" "ורדו" "rule over" and "conquer". At the time of its composition, this choice of words was prescient: it would be within the power of humanity to truly endanger other species and the habitability of Earth.

Rabbi Yehuda Loew of Prague, scholar and mystic in the 16th Century, links this passage on human power with the idea that we are made in the

---

12 Ramban on Genesis 1:26
13 Genesis 2:7
14 Genesis 1:28

15

image of G-d.[15] He suggests that, just as God is the Sovereign in the universe, human beings were granted a subsidiary sovereignty below on this earth. It was to be the domain for human possibility to perfect, to sustain, or to ruin this planet.

Rabbi Chaim of Volozhin, a revered Polish Talmudist and ethicist in the 18th and early 19th Century, similarly describes the immense power vested in humanity on this earth and even beyond, a frequent assertion among teachers of Kabbalah.

As it were, when God, may God be blessed, created Adam, God granted power over uncounted worlds and placed in human hands that humanity would speak and guide them (those worlds) by means of every detail of one's movements, deeds, spoken words, and thoughts and all the aspects of one's actions whether for good or for the opposite...Just as God, may God's Name be blessed, is Lord and all powerful for everything that exists in all worlds, ordering and leading them every minute according to the Divine will, thus God empowered Adam so that Adam would open and shut down uncounted powers and worlds by the agency of one's actions and endeavors every moment.[16]

Reb Chaim emphasizes that human power can be expressed in every aspect of one's life. Even gestures, speech, and thought are sources of one's power.

Scrolling fast forward to the 20th Century, Amos Oz, the exceptional modern Israeli writer, in 1981 spoke about the imprint of humanity on this earth:

And now it is my turn for a terrible confession. I object to nature preservation. The very ideal of "preservation" is not acceptable in almost any area of life. We have not come into this world to protect or preserve any given thing, mitzvot, the works of our ancestors, nature, or cultural

---

15 Rabbi Yehudah Loew of Prague, Derech Chayim, "Pirke Avot", 3:14
16 Rabbi Chayim of Voloshin, Nefesh HaChayim, Section 1, Chapter 3

heritage…We have not inherited a museum, to patiently wipe off the dust from its displays or to polish the glass… Nature also is not a museum. One is allowed to touch, allowed to move, to draw closer, to change and to leave our stamp…. Touch the stone. Touch the animal. Touch your fellow man. On one condition. How to touch? To answer "on one leg" and in a word, I would say: "with love".[17]

We inevitably touch the created world deeply.

It may well be an impossibility to imagine the human presence on earth without the exercise of power. The only question is whether that power is harnessed to a good end or leads to irreparable damage. Oz reminds us to touch the created world gently and with love.

Humanity's Connection to the Earth

The power vested in being human is quickly humbled when origins are considered. The Torah proclaims that every human being is bound to the soil of the Earth itself. Returning to the passage quoted above, we have learned that:

וַיִּיצֶר יְהֹוָה אֱלֹהִים אֶת־הָאָדָם עָפָר מִן־הָאֲדָמָה וַיִּפַּח בְּאַפָּיו נִשְׁמַת חַיִּים וַיְהִי הָאָדָם לְנֶפֶשׁ חַיָּה :

God formed the human from the dust of the earth, blowing into his nostrils the breath of life: the human became a living being.[18]

Later we are taught that we return to our origins when life ends, and we become dust once more. A human being is not a creature standing apart from nature but is instead thoroughly integrated with the earth itself, emerging from the dust, exercising power, then returning once more to dust, the place of our origin.

Chapter 2 in **Genesis** profoundly defines humanity's role. Adam is placed in the Garden of Eden with a specific purpose:

---

17 Oz, Amos, remarks in a speech in 1981. I am indebted to Professor Alon Tal for bringing this text to my attention.
18 Genesis 2:7

לעבדה ולשמרה.

To work it and to guard it.[19]

This mandate for the first human beings is understood as marching orders for all who follow. Our intended mission on planet Earth is to care for the Earth and its creatures. In fact, the Hebrew root meaning to work also means to "serve". This is then a call to serve as a sacred task. The same word in Hebrew is later used for service to God, underscoring the possibility of holiness in working the soil anywhere on Earth.

Rabbi Samson Raphael Hirsch, scholar and community leader in 19th Century Germany, teaches that the exercise of power had to be guided by moral standards:

The moral behavior of Adam and the responsible use that one does with the abundant natural world assists nature to progress in its purpose and enables it to continue to grow.[20]

Dr. Jeremy Benstein, senior staffer at the Heschel Center for Sustainability in Tel Aviv, translates the Hebrew in this phrase in contemporary terms to mean "sustainable development"[21]. He learns from the text the need to frame our "work" with guardrails so that the consequences of our actions do not bring destruction. Guarding places limits on our "work" so that we learn to respect boundaries.

Naming All Creatures

וַיִּצֶר יְהֹוָה אֱלֹהִים מִן־הָאֲדָמָה כָּל־חַיַּת הַשָּׂדֶה וְאֵת כָּל־עוֹף הַשָּׁמַיִם וַיָּבֵא אֶל־הָאָדָם לִרְאוֹת מַה־
יִּקְרָא־לוֹ וְכֹל אֲשֶׁר יִקְרָא־לוֹ הָאָדָם נֶפֶשׁ חַיָּה הוּא שְׁמוֹ:

And God formed out of the earth all the wild beasts and all the birds of the sky and brought them to the human to see what he would call t h e m ; a n d

---

19 Genesis 2:15

20 Hirsch, Rabbi Samson Raphael, Commentary on Genesis 2:15

21 Benstein, Jeremy, essayist in The Sacred Earth, (New York: Central Conference of America Rabbis, 2023), pp. 34-35

whatever the human called each living creature, that would be its name.[22]
Ever since creation, the human family has been assiduously assigning names
not only to new species of animals and plants but to land and bodies of water
and to virtually every place on Earth. Wherever we reach, we begin to name.

What is the significance of assigning a name? At the very least, it is a
sign that we have noticed a unique quality in that which we are naming and
that we wish to distinguish one creature, plant, or place from another. In a
deeper sense, when we name, we ascribe value and enter a relationship. To
give a name is to rescue anyone or anything from anonymity. The psalmist
considers naming a Divine act:

מוֹנֶה מִסְפָּר לַכּוֹכָבִים לְכֻלָּם שֵׁמוֹת יִקְרָא:

God reckoned the number of the stars;
to each gave its name.[23]

Giving names to countless stars implies that each one is unique and is
noticed. Similarly, naming on earth or in the heavens reflects the fact that a
creature or a facet of nature is accorded its own status. It is at least the first
step towards caring. Naming emulates God.

Naming a place previously without a name has even been used to stir
people to action when a natural habitat has been threatened. A well-chosen
name can become a catalyst to save a fragile environment or an endangered
species.[24]

Naming in Jewish tradition is sanctified at birth with a ceremony
declaring the newborn's Hebrew name. What is unique is that one's proper
name is immediately joined with the name of one's parents; for example, one
is called Isaac son of Abraham and Sarah. Traditionally the father's name
is linked to his progeny. In the modern era, the mother's name is more and

---

22 Genesis, 2:19
23 Psalms 147:4
24 https://www.israelgives.org/amuta/580528974

more frequently linked as well, a much-needed correction. When celebrating a milestone such as Bar or Bat Mitzvah, when one marries, and even at the end of life, a person's full name is used including one's parents. That full name is inscribed in documents, spoken aloud, and finally engraved on a tombstone. Whenever a person is honored by being called to the Torah in a synagogue service, he or she is summoned by one's complete name. A full name in Hebrew declares the connection of generations and implies the hope for continuity over time. An individual is never seen as severed from the chain of one's family and one's people. Building a more perfect world is the work of many generations. By carrying a name that includes two generations, Jews are taught that we are part of a long chain stretching into the past with an implied obligation to become a vital link into the future. No viable pathway into the future is possible without a healthy planet on which to work towards one's dreams and destiny.

The Earth Reacts to Human Folly

When Adam and Eve fail to uphold the one restriction they were given in the Garden of Eden by eating fruit from the Tree of Knowledge, there are severe consequences. The earth itself from which they were formed pushes back. Instead of the ease with which they had been able to sustain themselves from the produce of the soil, Adam and Eve must now work hard to nourish themselves. Even then, there is no guarantee of success:

וּלְאָדָם אָמַר כִּי־שָׁמַעְתָּ לְקוֹל אִשְׁתֶּךָ וַתֹּאכַל מִן־הָעֵץ אֲשֶׁר צִוִּיתִיךָ לֵאמֹר לֹא תֹאכַל מִמֶּנּוּ אֲרוּרָה הָאֲדָמָה בַּעֲבוּרֶךָ בְּעִצָּבוֹן תֹּאכֲלֶנָּה כֹּל יְמֵי חַיֶּיךָ:

To Adam [God] said, "Because you did as your wife said and ate of the tree about which I commanded you, 'You shall not eat of it,'
Cursed be the ground because of you;
By hard labor shall you eat of it
All the days of your life:

20

וְקוֹץ וְדַרְדַּר תַּצְמִיחַ לָךְ וְאָכַלְתָּ אֶת־עֵשֶׂב הַשָּׂדֶה:

Thorns and thistles shall it sprout for you.
But your food shall be the grasses of the field;

בְּזֵעַת אַפֶּיךָ תֹּאכַל לֶחֶם עַד שׁוּבְךָ אֶל־הָאֲדָמָה כִּי מִמֶּנָּה לֻקָּחְתָּ כִּי־עָפָר אַתָּה וְאֶל־עָפָר תָּשׁוּב:

By the sweat of your brow
Shall you get bread to eat,
Until you return to the ground –
For from it you were taken.
For dust you are,
And to dust you shall return." [25]

In this first instance of moral failure, we learn how the earth registers its protest. In consistent passages to follow, the earth is invested with personality and feelings. The moral tenor of human activity is reflected in the earth itself.

Human failure results in estrangement from the intimacy with the earth that had been originally posited. Thorns and thistles are the result of hard labor. Moral achievements could be seen in the soil's rich productivity, moral failures in that same soil's refusal to produce its best fruits. Once again, Adam and Eve are reminded of their origin and their destiny, emerging from and finally becoming one with the earth itself.

A few verses later, we learn of the first example of exile in Torah. No longer is the scene of disobedience in the Garden of Eden hospitable to the first couple. They must settle elsewhere to make a new beginning. The Torah explicitly points back to human origins in interpreting the need for exile:

וַיְשַׁלְּחֵהוּ יְהוָה אֱלֹהִים מִגַּן־עֵדֶן לַעֲבֹד אֶת־הָאֲדָמָה אֲשֶׁר לֻקַּח מִשָּׁם:

So God banished humankind from the garden of Eden, to till the soil from

---

25 Genesis 3:17-19

which it (humankind) was taken.[26]

Since Adam and Eve came from the earth itself, it is as though they have violated the very materials from which they were formed. They must move on because they had betrayed that place on Earth from which they were made.

The following chapter narrates the further steep decline in moral behavior when Cain slays his brother Abel in a moment of passion. The first murder recorded immediately opens an abyss between Cain and the earth itself:

וַיֹּאמֶר יְהֹוָה אֶל־קַיִן אֵי הֶבֶל אָחִיךָ וַיֹּאמֶר לֹא יָדַעְתִּי הֲשֹׁמֵר אָחִי אָנֹכִי:

God said to Cain, "Where is your brother Abel?" And he said, "I do not know. Am I my brother's keeper?"

וַיֹּאמֶר מֶה עָשִׂיתָ קוֹל דְּמֵי אָחִיךָ צֹעֲקִים אֵלַי מִן־הָאֲדָמָה:

God said: "What have you done? Hark, your brother's blood cries out to Me from the ground!

וְעַתָּה אָרוּר אָתָּה מִן־הָאֲדָמָה אֲשֶׁר פָּצְתָה אֶת־פִּיהָ לָקַחַת אֶת־דְּמֵי אָחִיךָ מִיָּדֶךָ:

"Therefore, you shall be cursed from the ground, which opened its mouth to receive your brother's blood from your hand.

כִּי תַעֲבֹד אֶת־הָאֲדָמָה לֹא־תֹסֵף תֵּת־כֹּחָהּ לָךְ נָע וָנָד תִּהְיֶה בָאָרֶץ:

"If you till the soil, it shall no longer yield its strength to you. You shall become a ceaseless wanderer on earth."[27]

In response to this most grievous of sins, the murder of a fellow human, the earth "opens its mouth to receive" Abels's blood and then refuses to grow plants to nourish Cain. In fact, **no place** on earth will provide a home for him. He would be an alien, totally estranged from the earth, ever a wanderer, never finding a compatible place to live. It seems that every

---

26 Genesis 3:23
27 Genesis 4:9-12

22

human transgression results in estrangement from the land itself, with the seriousness of the offense linked to proportional punishment. A person and the Earth had to be in harmony to co-exist.

In the modern period, human action has left its damaging mark on the land itself by degrading and eroding the soil, promoting desertification, and continual deforesting. Hurting the earth and humanity march hand in hand.

Exile in Jewish History

The consequences of sin which afflicted Adam, Eve, and their son Cain become a prologue to the destiny of the Jewish people. "Exile" is a painfully etched word in the annals of Jewish history. The consensus of rabbinic sages is that exile did not simply happen to the Jews who were victimized by a succession of conquering empires. The catastrophes remembered vividly over time are consistently attributed to the Jewish people's own moral failings which severed their inner cohesion and strength and made them more vulnerable to attack from without.

וּמִפְּנֵי חֲטָאֵינוּ גָּלִינוּ מֵאַרְצֵנוּ.

Due to our sins, we were exiled from the land.[28]

Once again, the land is personified. The earth cannot bear the presence of serious human failings. Even, perhaps especially, if that land is the "promised" land of Israel, upholding the commandments is the condition for continuity in settlement. When serious transgressions were committed, the land could no longer abide the presence of those who had transgressed. When idolatry or baseless hatred reigned, the land reacted. The empires of Assyria, Babylonia, and Rome, which conquered the land and destroyed the sacred sanctuaries in Jerusalem, seem to be agents of the land itself. The people had to settle elsewhere. In the future, they would need to atone to have the right to return and to rebuild.

---

28 From the liturgy of the Musaf (Additional) service on major festivals in the Jewish calendar

What becomes very clear in the eyes of the Biblical writer is that the niche of the human family in the ecosystem of the Earth is rooted in adherence to basic moral standards. The condition of the Earth is seen as a litmus test for human moral compliance. While, as in our time, human culpability is coupled with the assault on the Earth itself, the Torah's view expresses a much broader moral sensibility of the Earth.

The Flood

The reaction of nature to sin on an even grander scale is apparent in the generation of the flood.

וַתִּשָּׁחֵת הָאָרֶץ לִפְנֵי הָאֱלֹהִים וַתִּמָּלֵא הָאָרֶץ חָמָס:

The earth was destroyed before God; the earth was filled with violence.[29]
Of special note is the repeated assertion that the "Earth was destroyed", and the cause was human violence.

וַיַּרְא אֱלֹהִים אֶת־הָאָרֶץ וְהִנֵּה נִשְׁחָתָה כִּי־הִשְׁחִית כָּל־בָּשָׂר אֶת־דַּרְכּוֹ עַל־הָאָרֶץ:

And God saw how the earth was destroyed, for all flesh had corrupted its ways on earth.[30]
So close is the relationship between Noah's generation and the Earth itself that the transgressions of people are marked immediately on the surface of the planet. According to a curious midrash[31] linked to the words "the earth was destroyed", the flood effectively washed away the soil to a depth of three handbreadths, the place to which the plow reaches. The implication is that wherever the human hand touched, there would be destruction. The fate of the Earth was coextensive with human reach.

When the Earth was filled with violence, there is no solid ground on which human beings can stand. Everything is out of balance. As rain falls

---

29 Genesis 6:11
30 Genesis 6:12
31 B'reshet Rabbah ,"Noach", 31 Midrashic literature encompasses a vast array of early commentary on Torah.

incessantly, it's as if creation is unravelling, dry land disappearing and a return to the darkness and chaos preceding creation. The land upon which plants, animals, and humans can thrive is out of reach. The only survivors are those who were righteous, protected in the Ark despite the pervading culture of crime.

In one sense, the flood story is closest to this time of climate change. The tale encompasses the entire planet which was totally without a moral compass. Today's crisis also encircles the world. It is due to human folly and disregard for the limits of human consumption and the abuse of nature's riches.

In the Torah when the flood recedes, God makes a promise to the survivors:

עֹד כָּל־יְמֵי הָאָרֶץ זֶרַע וְקָצִיר וְקֹר וָחֹם וְקַיִץ וָחֹרֶף וְיוֹם וָלַיְלָה לֹא יִשְׁבֹּתוּ:

"So long as the Earth endures
Seedtime and harvest,
Cold and heat,
Summer and winter,
Day and night
Shall not cease."[32]

This promise of healthy natural cycles is premised on the endurance of the Earth itself. God made this solemn promise of continuity in natural rhythms. These gifts, however, are conditioned on avoiding the loss of the Earth caused by the relentless assault on its viability by the human family. On this theme much more will follow in the pages ahead.

Abraham and Sarah's Promise From God

When Abraham and Sarah hear from God that they must begin a journey away from their ancestral home, they are directed to journey west to

---

32 Genesis 8:22

a new land that will ultimately become the home for them and their promised descendants:

וַיֹּאמֶר יְהֹוָה אֶל־אַבְרָם לֶךְ־לְךָ מֵאַרְצְךָ וּמִמּוֹלַדְתְּךָ וּמִבֵּית אָבִיךָ אֶל־הָאָרֶץ אֲשֶׁר אַרְאֶךָּ:

God said to Abram, "Go forth from your native land and from your father's house to the land that I will show you.

וְאֶעֶשְׂךָ לְגוֹי גָּדוֹל וַאֲבָרֶכְךָ וַאֲגַדְּלָה שְׁמֶךָ וֶהְיֵה בְּרָכָה:

"I will make of you a great nation,
And I will bless you;
I will make your name great,
And you shall be a blessing.

וַאֲבָרְכָה מְבָרְכֶיךָ וּמְקַלֶּלְךָ אָאֹר וְנִבְרְכוּ בְךָ כֹּל מִשְׁפְּחֹת הָאֲדָמָה:

"I will bless those who bless you
And curse the one who curses you;
And all the families of the earth
Shall bless themselves by you."[33]

For everything to unfold as God envisioned, this couple will need an enduring stage on which to live and grow. Their destiny will impact the entire world, but it will take shape primarily in one modest land. Going to and from that land informs much of the narrative in **Genesis**. We learn of the first foothold in Canaan when Abraham purchases a burial plot for Sarah. From the beginning of the book of **Exodus** until the end of Torah, the direction of movement of the entire Jewish people is unstintingly towards that promised land. Pointing towards that land then became a constant motif from every corner of the diaspora. Clearly the promise of the Jewish future needed a parcel of earth on which to flourish. That promised land and the Jewish future are inextricably bound together.

It is notable that when the promise of a great future is first given,

---

33 Genesis 12:1-3

Abraham and Sarah are a childless couple. They are told that their descendants will be as numerous as the stars in the sky or as the grains of sand by the sea. To accomplish this goal, they first need to give birth to at least one child. Then they will need faith that untold generations will follow. On children, grandchildren, and great grandchildren, their hope rested. They needed a sustainable future. Their destiny encompassing a project of uncounted generations. לדור ודור , from generation to generation, became a beloved watchword to this day. For this promise to be fulfilled, sustainability is essential. For Jewish dreams to become a reality, the Jews need a healthy place on Earth. Jewish sustainability is surely dependent on the sustainability of the Earth itself.

Every human life needs a place to thrive, to call home. For the Jewish people collectively, such a place is needed, too. Since Jewish destiny was linked to a way of life guided by ethical and spiritual values, it will become optimally manifest in a parcel of earth, a homeland. Jewish living emphasizes the doing of Mitzvot, commandments which govern virtually every aspect of life. These Mitzvot require concrete actions and an arena where they become visible, a home, a community, a city, a land. For a society, a people, to demonstrate to the world the ideal to which it is called, it needs a place called home.

CHAPTER TWO

EXODUS

The Sabbath

In Jewish tradition, rich in commandments, the Sabbath stands out. Long before it was inscribed in the Ten Commandments, it was mysteriously known and even imprinted in the natural cycle of work and rest. God rested on the seventh day and declared it "holy". It was the first manifestation of the concept of holiness in Torah. Time could be sanctified.

When the Jewish people are liberated from Egypt and need sustenance in the wilderness before reaching Mount Sinai, they are given manna each day to eat. While the people are instructed to gather only enough manna each day for their needs on that day alone, they are told that they should collect twice as much on Friday to provide for two days, Friday and the Sabbath. No manna will be given on the Sabbath itself. On the seventh day, even before the revelation at Sinai, Sabbath rules were operative. Moses had to personally teach that commandment immediately after the exodus:

וַיֹּאמֶר מֹשֶׁה אִכְלֻהוּ הַיּוֹם כִּי־שַׁבָּת הַיּוֹם לַיהוָה הַיּוֹם לֹא תִמְצָאֻהוּ בַּשָּׂדֶה׃

Then Moses said, *"Eat it today, for today is a Sabbath of God; you will not find it today on the plain.*

שֵׁשֶׁת יָמִים תִּלְקְטֻהוּ וּבַיּוֹם הַשְּׁבִיעִי שַׁבָּת לֹא יִהְיֶה־בּוֹ׃

Six days you shall gather it; on the seventh day, the Sabbath, there will be none."[34]

What is it about the Sabbath that lends it such centrality in Jewish life, and what is it about the Sabbath that speaks more generally to the climate crisis? Abraham Joshua Heschel presciently addresses this subject:

---

34 Exodus 16:25-26

In the language of the Bible, the world was brought into being in the six days of creation, yet its survival depends upon the holiness of the seventh day. Great are the laws that govern the processes of nature. Yet without holiness there would be neither greatness nor nature.[35]

How does this seventh day and its holiness relate to world survival? How does the survivability of nature depend on the Sabbath?

Jewish law governing the Sabbath is the most elaborately developed of any mitzvah.

זָכוֹר אֶת־יוֹם הַשַּׁבָּת לְקַדְּשׁוֹ:

Remember the sabbath day and keep it holy.

שֵׁשֶׁת יָמִים תַּעֲבֹד וְעָשִׂיתָ כָּל־מְלַאכְתֶּךָ:

Six days you shall labor and do all your work,

וְיוֹם הַשְּׁבִיעִי שַׁבָּת לַיהוָה אֱלֹהֶיךָ לֹא־תַעֲשֶׂה כָל־מְלָאכָה אַתָּה וּבִנְךָ־וּבִתֶּךָ עַבְדְּךָ וַאֲמָתְךָ וּבְהֶמְתֶּךָ וְגֵרְךָ אֲשֶׁר בִּשְׁעָרֶיךָ:

but the seventh day is a sabbath of your God: you shall not do any work – you, your son or daughter, your male or female slave, or your cattle, or the stranger who is within your settlements.

כִּי שֵׁשֶׁת־יָמִים עָשָׂה יְהוָה אֶת־הַשָּׁמַיִם וְאֶת־הָאָרֶץ אֶת־הַיָּם וְאֶת־כָּל־אֲשֶׁר־בָּם וַיָּנַח בַּיּוֹם הַשְּׁבִיעִי עַל־כֵּן בֵּרַךְ יְהוָה אֶת־יוֹם הַשַּׁבָּת וַיְקַדְּשֵׁהוּ: {ס}

For in six days God made heaven and earth and sea – and all that is in them – and then rested on the seventh day; therefore, God blessed the sabbath day and hallowed it.[36]

From these four verses, emerged an amazing, intricate structure, a cathedral in time rather than in space.

---

35 Heschel, Abraham Joshua, The Sabbath, (New York: Farrar, Straus, and Young, 1951), p. 76
36 Exodus 20:8-11

The details are immense. From the prohibition of work in the Ten Commandments, rabbinic sages developed a definition of work and derived 39 categories of labor to be avoided. They include most of what would be considered work by any definition, but there is more. Not only was the mistress or the master of the household to refrain from work. Every person living in one's domain or service is to rest. Even animals should relish a day without labor. Control over others is suspended.

Another restriction related to travel. Movement from place to place is very limited on Shabbat. In many communities, travel by car or any mode of transport is suspended. Food that is to be consumed on Shabbat must be gathered and prepared in advance. No cooking can take place. Most notably, virtually nothing can be transported from place to place, symbolic of the transfer of goods and services that characterize commerce in any time or place. And no living thing, plant or animal, can be harmed on the day of rest. For those who keep Shabbat, even swatting a mosquito is forbidden. Not even a leaf can be torn from a tree or bush. This is a day when all species experience no trace of violence or manipulation by human hands at least. Humility is nurtured as control over any other is relinquished.

The underlying principle for these prohibitions is that once each week we pull back from causing any change in the world. We neither create nor destroy. Instead, we are completely at peace with creation. We exercise no control, exert no power. The limited power that was granted to humankind to conquer, rule, and shape the world is suspended. It is a sacred time to realize anew that we are not the owners of the earth on which we live. For six days, we often vigorously use that power we were granted. On the Sabbath, we step back humbly and take stock of what we have done. It is hoped that we admit our limits and acknowledge our Creator as the Owner of this Earth. We are its servants, its guardians. When Heschel writes that nature would cease to exist without the Sabbath, he teaches that human power unleashed without humility could result in untold damage to creation. In subsequent passages of Torah, we will see further periodic and dramatic limitations of human power. Yet the Sabbath is the most potent as it recurs every week without pause.

The Rockefeller Center in New York once belonged to the Rockefeller family. It was turned over to the city of New York for the benefit of its citizens. Yet one day each year, it was shut down in acknowledgement of its owner. On that day, it was closed to public use. On that day, New Yorkers had a gentle reminder that they are not in charge. Similarly, the Sabbath with its many precepts limiting any behavior that implies mastery is a dramatic reminder of human status. We are not the possessors of this Earth. We are its custodians.

With the Sabbath seen in this light, it may be the most powerful practice in Jewish tradition to foster awareness of our place on this Earth and of our need to be responsible stewards. One day each week, the carbon footprint of one who is Sabbath observant disappears or is at least minimized. Yet its most critical power is the effect it might have on the other six days when we return to our accustomed tasks. When human power is restored on Saturday night, will it be exercised with care, compassion, and humility?

Emulating Creation: Building the Tabernacle

There were three major achievements of the people of Israel at the dawn of their history. They gained liberation from Egyptian slavery; they received the Ten Commandments and more at Mount Sinai; and they built the Tabernacle at the center of their camp to nurtures access to the Divine Presence and to offer their service.

The building project occupies much of the last half of the book of **Exodus**. Each step is told and retold in exacting detail. Commentators ancient and modern have noted especially the striking parallels in the use of key words between creating the Tabernacle and the creation of the world. For example, note the similarities in language between **Genesis** and **Exodus**:

וַיַּרְא אֱלֹהִים אֶת־כָּל־אֲשֶׁר עָשָׂה וְהִנֵּה־טוֹב מְאֹד וַיְהִי־עֶרֶב וַיְהִי־בֹקֶר יוֹם הַשִּׁשִּׁי:

And God saw all that had been made and found it very good. And there was evening and there was morning, the sixth day.[37]

וַיַּרְא מֹשֶׁה אֶת־כָּל־הַמְּלָאכָה וְהִנֵּה עָשׂוּ אֹתָהּ כַּאֲשֶׁר צִוָּה יְהֹוָה כֵּן עָשׂוּ וַיְבָרֶךְ אֹתָם מֹשֶׁה:

And when Moses saw that they had performed all the tasks – as God had commanded, so they had done – Moses blessed them.[38]

And again, at the completion of each project, the careful choice of words connects the two events:

וַיְכֻלּוּ הַשָּׁמַיִם וְהָאָרֶץ וְכָל־צְבָאָם:

The heaven and the earth were finished, and all their array.[39]

וַתֵּכֶל כָּל־עֲבֹדַת מִשְׁכַּן אֹהֶל מוֹעֵד וַיַּעֲשׂוּ בְּנֵי יִשְׂרָאֵל כְּכֹל אֲשֶׁר צִוָּה יְהֹוָה אֶת־מֹשֶׁה כֵּן עָשׂוּ: {פ}

Thus was completed all the work of the Tabernacle of the Tent of Meeting. The Israelites did so; just as God had commanded Moses, so they did.[40]

וַיְכַל אֱלֹהִים בַּיּוֹם הַשְּׁבִיעִי מְלַאכְתּוֹ אֲשֶׁר עָשָׂה וַיִּשְׁבֹּת בַּיּוֹם הַשְּׁבִיעִי מִכָּל־מְלַאכְתּוֹ אֲשֶׁר עָשָׂה:

On the seventh day God finished the work that had been undertaken: [God] ceased on the seventh day from doing any of the work.[41]

וַיְכַל מֹשֶׁה אֶת־הַמְּלָאכָה:

And Moses had finished the work.[42]

---

37 Genesis, 1:31
38 Exodus 39:43
39 Genesis 2:1
40 Exodus 39:32
41 Genesis 2:2
42 Exodus 40:33

וַיְבָ֤רֶךְ אֱלֹהִים֙ אֶת־י֣וֹם הַשְּׁבִיעִ֔י וַיְקַדֵּ֖שׁ אֹת֑וֹ כִּ֣י ב֤וֹ שָׁבַת֙ מִכָּל־מְלַאכְתּ֔וֹ אֲשֶׁר־בָּרָ֥א אֱלֹהִ֖ים לַעֲשֽׂוֹת׃

And God blessed the seventh day and declared it holy *– having ceased on it from all the work of creation that God had done.*[43]

וַיַּ֨רְא מֹשֶׁ֜ה אֶת־כָּל־הַמְּלָאכָ֗ה וְהִנֵּה֙ עָשׂ֣וּ אֹתָ֔הּ כַּאֲשֶׁ֛ר צִוָּ֥ה יְהֹוָ֖ה כֵּ֣ן עָשׂ֑וּ וַיְבָ֥רֶךְ אֹתָ֖ם מֹשֶֽׁה׃

And when Moses saw that they had performed all the tasks – as יהוה *had commanded, so they had done –* ***Moses blessed them.***[44]

וְלָקַחְתָּ֙ אֶת־שֶׁ֣מֶן הַמִּשְׁחָ֔ה וּמָשַׁחְתָּ֥ אֶת־הַמִּשְׁכָּ֖ן וְאֶת־כָּל־אֲשֶׁר־בּ֑וֹ וְקִדַּשְׁתָּ֥ אֹת֛וֹ וְאֶת־כָּל־כֵּלָ֖יו וְהָ֥יָה קֹֽדֶשׁ׃

You shall take the anointing oil and anoint the Tabernacle and all that is in it ***to consecrate it and all its furnishings, so that it shall be holy.***[45]

It was understood that the creation of the world and the construction of the Tabernacle were to be seen as bound together. Usage of identical or similar words or phrases from one passage in the text to another was a literary way the Biblical writer connected the texts. Creation was God's work. The Tabernacle was to be a human act of creation emulating in miniature the cosmic act of God.

What could this mean? For much of human history leading to this moment in the wilderness, the human project of God had been one failure after another. Even in the wilderness, the worship of the golden calf almost signaled an end of the Jewish people. The estrangement of the people from God and from the Earth had reached a breaking point.

The Tabernacle was intended to make a new beginning with a new symbolic rebuilding of the world. The Kli Yakar, Shlomo Ephraim ben Aaron Luntschitz who lived in Prague in the 17th century, interprets the parallels:

וכמו שמצינו במעשה בראשית שנאמר בכל מלאכה כי טוב ובסוף אמר וירא אלהים את כל אשר עשה

והנה טוב (שם א לא), כי יש לך דברים שהם טובים כשהם כל אחד בפני עצמו אבל כשהם מעורבים

---

43 Genesis 2:3
44 Exodus 39:43
45 Exodus 40:9

יחד אינן טובים כי אין זיווגם עולה יפה, על כן אמר במעשה בראשית שכולם היו טובים כשהיו כל
אחד מהם בעצמם דהיינו טוב פרטי, ואחר כך אמר שגם טוב כללי היה בהם כי גם אחר שנתחברו כולם
יחד היה חיבורם טוב לכך חזר ואמר וירא אלהים את כל אשר עשה והנה טוב מאד. כך בעבודת
המשכן מתחילה אמר ותכל כל עבודת משכן אוהל העדות ויעשו בני ישראל ככל אשר צוה ה' את משה
כן עשו, שמשמע שכל אחד בפני עצמו נעשה כאשר צוה ה' את משה, אבל עדיין לא פורש שאחר
שנעשה הכל אז סדרו את כל עבודה ועבודה על מקומו המיוחד לו דהיינו טוב כללי, על כן חזר ואמר
ככל אשר צוה ה' את משה כן עשו בני ישראל את כל העבודה, כי היה בהם טוב כללי שנעשו על הסדר
הנכון דהיינו חיבור כל העבודה ביחד.

*Just as we found in the work of creation as it is said after the completion
of each stage that it was good, and in the end "God saw all that God had
made and it was very good". For there are things that are good when
considered each one by itself, but when they are joined together, they are
not good because they do not fit together well. Therefore (God) said in the
work of creation that they were all good when each one (was considered)
individually, thus "good" by itself; and afterwards, (God) said that they
were also good together; for after they were joined they fit well. Thus (God)
added: "And God saw all that God had done and it was very good."*

*Similarly in building the Tabernacle, at the outset it was said: "All
of the work of the Tabernacle, the tent of meeting, was finished, and the
Children of Israel did exactly as God commanded Moses", meaning that
each task individually was accomplished as God had commanded Moses.
Yet it was not yet explained that after everything was complete, they ordered
every facet to be in its designated place, meaning the collective good.
Therefore, (God) came back and said (again): "Just as God had commanded
Moses, so the Israelites had done all the work" because the general good
was accomplished for they were assembled in the proper order meaning the
connection of all the work together.[46]*

---

46 Kli Yakar, on Exodus, "Pekudey", 39:43

The Jewish people created an echo of the creation narrative.

Creation was infinitely variegated with abundant species on earth and in the seas. Separately each specific creation was magnificent and declared to be "good". Would such a rich world of differences work together to form an integrated natural world of beauty? Would there be a smoothly functioning ecosystem? The declaration on the sixth day that all was "very good" testified to the integrity of the whole: everything together received higher praise than each received as a separate entity.

Rabbinic reading of the building of the Tabernacle suggests that, despite the myriad of skills required, the many different materials used, the precise measurements required, the number of sacred objects and spaces needed, and the sheer scope of the project, the result was one, integrated, cohesive structure. Just as each object and space were executed according to plan, the whole was likewise "very good."

The nation had demonstrated that they can create a new world in miniature and begin anew. What is very notable in the process of assembling the Tabernacle is that participants willingly volunteered their time and skills and contributed their resources virtually without limit.

וַיִּקְחוּ מִלִּפְנֵי מֹשֶׁה אֵת כָּל־הַתְּרוּמָה אֲשֶׁר הֵבִיאוּ בְּנֵי יִשְׂרָאֵל לִמְלֶאכֶת עֲבֹדַת הַקֹּדֶשׁ לַעֲשֹׂת אֹתָהּ וְהֵם הֵבִיאוּ אֵלָיו עוֹד נְדָבָה בַּבֹּקֶר בַּבֹּקֶר:

They (the artisans) took over from Moses all the gifts that the Israelites had brought, to carry out the tasks connected with the service of the sanctuary. But when these continued to bring freewill offerings to him morning after morning,

וַיָּבֹאוּ כָּל־הַחֲכָמִים הָעֹשִׂים אֵת כָּל־מְלֶאכֶת הַקֹּדֶשׁ אִישׁ־אִישׁ מִמְּלַאכְתּוֹ אֲשֶׁר־הֵמָּה עֹשִׂים:

all the sages who were engaged in the tasks of the sanctuary came, from the task upon which each one was engaged,

36

וַיֹּאמְרוּ אֶל־מֹשֶׁה לֵּאמֹר מַרְבִּים הָעָם לְהָבִיא מִדֵּי הָעֲבֹדָה לַמְּלָאכָה אֲשֶׁר־צִוָּה יְהֹוָה לַעֲשֹׂת אֹתָהּ:

and said to Moses, "The people are bringing more than is needed for the tasks entailed in the work that God has commanded to be done."

וַיְצַו מֹשֶׁה וַיַּעֲבִירוּ קוֹל בַּמַּחֲנֶה לֵאמֹר אִישׁ וְאִשָּׁה אַל־יַעֲשׂוּ־עוֹד מְלָאכָה לִתְרוּמַת הַקֹּדֶשׁ וַיִּכָּלֵא הָעָם מֵהָבִיא:

Moses thereupon had this proclamation made throughout the camp: "Let no man or woman make further effort toward gifts for the sanctuary!" So the people stopped bringing:

וְהַמְּלָאכָה הָיְתָה דַיָּם לְכָל־הַמְּלָאכָה לַעֲשׂוֹת אֹתָהּ וְהוֹתֵר: {ס}

their efforts had been more than enough for all the tasks to be done.[47]

In this account, there is no sign of rancor or divisiveness. For a people accustomed to anger, complaints, and divisions, this seamless spectacle of an entire people working in harmony is remarkable. People of every age and gender worked easily and devotedly together. The sanctuary they created provided a pathway to atonement for the past and towards making a new beginning. They engaged in an act of personal and communal re-creation.

The Tabernacle stands as a powerful symbol of the power granted to humanity to build and rebuild a new world. Toward that end, all must have the will to work together and to take care that each part in this complex and magnificent ecosystem fits perfectly into the whole. Implicit in such an achievement is that each individual works not only within his or her self-interest but rather has in mind the welfare of the whole. In this way, estrangement from God and from the Earth itself n be overcome. Today, the success of that ancient building project accomplished by one small people stands as a summons for all people to join in an act of re-creation. This narrative is a symbol of hope that such a herculean task is possible. The last portion of the book of **Exodus** reaches back to the first word of **Genesis,**

---

47 Exodus 36:3-7

בראשית, "with (the possibility of) beginning (anew)." It reaffirms that this world is malleable enough that it can be re-created. Estrangement can be overcome; monumental transgression can yield to a fresh start.

Even the global threat to planet Earth can yield to human ingenuity and cooperation.

CHAPTER THREE

LEVITICUS

The Land Reacts Strongly to Human Misconduct

The book of **Leviticus** continues the theme of deep interconnectivity between human behavior and the earth itself. In Chapter 18, we read a list of grave moral failings that caused the land to reject its previous inhabitants:

וַתִּטְמָא הָאָרֶץ וָאֶפְקֹד עֲוֺנָהּ עָלֶיהָ וַתָּקִא הָאָרֶץ אֶת־יֹשְׁבֶיהָ:

Thus, the land became defiled; and I called it to account for its iniquity, and the land spewed out its inhabitants.

וּשְׁמַרְתֶּם אַתֶּם אֶת־חֻקֹּתַי וְאֶת־מִשְׁפָּטַי וְלֹא תַעֲשׂוּ מִכֹּל הַתּוֹעֵבֹת הָאֵלֶּה הָאֶזְרָח וְהַגֵּר הַגָּר בְּתוֹכְכֶם:

But you must keep My laws and My rules, and you must not do any of those abhorrent things, neither the citizen nor the stranger who resides among you;

כִּי אֶת־כָּל־הַתּוֹעֵבֹת הָאֵל עָשׂוּ אַנְשֵׁי־הָאָרֶץ אֲשֶׁר לִפְנֵיכֶם וַתִּטְמָא הָאָרֶץ:

for all those abhorrent things were done by the people who were in the land before you, and the land became defiled.

וְלֹא־תָקִיא הָאָרֶץ אֶתְכֶם בְּטַמַּאֲכֶם אֹתָהּ כַּאֲשֶׁר קָאָה אֶת־הַגּוֹי אֲשֶׁר לִפְנֵיכֶם:

So let not the land spew you out for defiling it, as it spewed out the nation that came before you.[48]

The land is anthropomorphized. It cannot abide in the presence of gross immorality; it is "defiled" by human activity. It reacts violently by "vomiting out" those who have transgressed. The nations that preceded Israel on the land were expelled for their bad behavior. The Israelites are equally at risk should they fall short. Any sojourn will be conditional.

In his classic work, *The Sand County Almanac*, environmentalist

---

48 rf Leviticus 18:25-28

Aldo Leopold writes of a new approach to ethics. Generally, ethics applies primarily to interhuman behavior and extends to the world of animals as well. He recommends adopting a similar connection to the land:

All ethics so far evolved rest upon a single premise: that the individual is a member of a community of interdependent parts. His instincts prompt him to compete for his place in that community, but his ethics prompt him to co-operate (perhaps in order that there may be a place to compete for.)

The land ethic simply enlarges the boundaries of the community to include soils, waters, plants, and animals, or, collectively, the land...

In short, a land ethic changes the role of homo sapiens from conqueror of the land-community to plain member and citizen of it. It implies respect for his fellow-members, and also respect for the community as such.[49]

The Torah's anthropomorphizing of the land endows it with a voice and a right to partnership. It is not simply a tool for human achievement. It presents itself as a living organism which deserves to be treated with dignity. There are clearly boundaries which the human family must respect in order that there be harmony and a sustained and shared co-existence between humanity and land.

Leopold continues:

That man is, in fact, only a member of a biotic team is shown by an ecological interpretation of history. Many historical events, hitherto explained solely in terms of human enterprise, were actually biotic interactions between people and land. The characteristics of the land determined the facts quite as potently as the characteristics of the men who lived on it.[50]

Leopold continues with a vivid example of significant effect of the

---

49 Leopold, Aldo, The Sand County Almanac and Other Writings on Conservation, (New York: The Library of America, 2013), pp. 172-173

50 Ibid, p. 173

land itself on historical events that would take place upon it:

Consider, for example, the settlement of the Mississippi valley. In the years following the Revolution, three groups were contending for its control: the native Indian, the French and English traders, and the American settlers. Historians wonder what would have happened if the English at Detroit had thrown a little more weight into the Indian side of those tipsy scales which decided the outcome of the colonial migration into the cane-lands of Kentucky. It is time now to ponder the fact that the cane-lands, when subjected to the particular mixture of forces represented by the cow, plow, fire, and axe of the pioneer, became bluegrass. What if the plant succession inherent in this dark and bloody ground had, under the impact of these forces, given us some worthless sedge, shrub, or weed? Would Boone and Kenton have held out? Would there have been any overflow into Ohio, Indiana, Illinois, and Missouri? Any Louisiana Purchase? Any transcontinental union of new states? Any Civil War?[51]

Aldo Leopold's enlargement of the proper realm of ethics to include all species and the land seemingly maps with the Torah's view of peaceful habitation and exile. The land has standing; the land has rights that deserve protection. Historic events can be seen as a breakdown in that human-land relationship. When moral standards with this expanded scope are honored, life can be stable and thrive. When they are violated, it is time to find another home. Facing a world awash with climate refugees, it seems proper to ask if our global moral compass is askew.

There is a major difference, however, in the nature and scope of moral behavior. For Leopold, how soil, water, and air are treated directly determines how people will fare with them. From the perspective of Torah, all aspects of human behavior will make their mark on the land. The violation of obligations in any relationship affects the land. Interpersonal sin, falling

---

51 Ibid, pp. 173-174

short in our relationship to the animal and plant world, and transgression in the Divine-human realm can upset the relationship to the land. Moral failure which does not damage the soil directly in any way can still become the trigger for exile and the search for a new home.

Respecting Boundaries of the Incomprehensible

While most mitzvot are transparent to reason, there are a small but significant number that seem to defy reason. They are called "chukim." Leviticus lists some of them:

אֶת־חֻקֹּתַי֮ תִּשְׁמֹ֒רוּ֒ בְּהֶמְתְּךָ֙ לֹא־תַרְבִּ֣יעַ כִּלְאַ֔יִם שָׂדְךָ֖ לֹא־תִזְרַ֣ע כִּלְאָ֑יִם וּבֶ֤גֶד כִּלְאַ֙יִם֙ שַֽׁעַטְנֵ֔ז לֹ֥א יַעֲלֶ֖ה עָלֶֽיךָ׃

You shall observe My laws. You shall not let your cattle mate with a different kind; you shall not sow your field with two kinds of seed; you shall not put on cloth from a mixture of two kinds of material.[52]

The Ramban, Rabbi Moshe Ben Nachman, noted commentator of the thirteenth century, teaches that what binds these different commandments together are boundaries in nature that should be respected.[53] Animals of different species should not mate with one another. A field should be planted with one kind of seed. A garment should not be made of an animal product and plant material within one weave. One of the most well-known chukim is "shatnez" which forbids wearing any article of clothing in which wool and linen are woven together joining an animal and a plant-based product. Jews who observe the laws strictly are taught that whether these natural boundaries are understood or not, they should be observed.

Rabbi Samson Raphael Hirsch, exceptional leader and scholar in 19th Century Germany, concurs when he teaches:

The same thoughtful regard you show to man, show as well to every lower being, to the earth which bears and sustains all; to the world of

---

52   Leviticus 19:19
53   Ramban on Leviticus 19:19

42

animals and plants...They (the chukim) ask of you to regard all things as God's possessions; destroy none; abuse none; waste nothing; employ all things wisely; the kinds and species of plants and animals are God's order; mingle them not. All creatures are servants in the household of creation. Respect even the feelings and desires of beasts.[54]

That we do not understand God's order is not a reason to ignore it. Aldo Leopold makes a strong point of the need to admit the limits of our knowledge:

The ordinary citizen assumes that science knows what makes the community clock tick; the scientist is equally sure that he does not.[55]

In a moving essay by Rabbi Joseph B. Soloveichik (eminent 20th Century theologian and scholar) entitled "Majesty and Humility," we learn of a deeply ingrained pattern in Jewish thought: the dialectic between the powers that are within human capacity and limitations on those powers. One of those powers is the ability to learn and to understand. Over and against this formidable power of intellect are the limits to our knowing. There are great mysteries that elude comprehensibility. In Soloveichik's words:

What does man cherish more than the intellect, around which his sense of dignity is centered? Precisely because of the supremacy of the intellect in human life, the Torah requires, at times, the suspension of the authority logos. Man defeats himself by accepting norms that the intellect cannot assimilate into its normative system. The Judaic concept of "chok" (singular form of a law without a discernable reason) represents human surrender and human defeat. Man, an intellectual being, ignores the logos and burdens himself with laws whose rational motif he cannot grasp.[56]

Accepting human limits, humility in the face of our frequent inability to

---

54 Hirsch, Rabbi Samson Raphael, Rav Hirsch's Nineteen Letters, (Translation by Bernard Drachman), Letter 11
55 Op. Cit., Léopold, Aldo, p,173
56 Soloveichik, Rabbi Joseph B., "Tradition", Spring 1978, "Majesty and Humility"

understand, is the antidote to the very human tendency to become overbearing and proud.

Who Owns the Land?

Near the conclusion of **Leviticus,** Torah turns its attention to how the land itself is to be treated. The land ethic takes center stage. The theme was first raised dramatically with the commandment to observe the Sabbath. While the weekly return of the Sabbath required a steady rhythm of pulling back from the exercise of control over the land and the world around oneself, this was only the beginning of teaching humility vis a vis the Earth and its gifts. Truly dramatic restraint is envisioned with an entire Sabbatical Year every seven years and a Jubilee Year each half century.

שֵׁשׁ שָׁנִים֙ תִּזְרַ֣ע שָׂדֶ֔ךָ וְשֵׁ֥שׁ שָׁנִ֖ים תִּזְמֹ֣ר כַּרְמֶ֑ךָ וְאָסַפְתָּ֖ אֶת־תְּבוּאָתָֽהּ׃

Six years you may sow your field and six years you may prune your vineyard and gather in the yield.

וּבַשָּׁנָ֣ה הַשְּׁבִיעִ֗ת שַׁבַּ֤ת שַׁבָּתוֹן֙ יִהְיֶ֣ה לָאָ֔רֶץ שַׁבָּ֖ת לַיהוָ֑ה שָׂדְךָ֙ לֹ֣א תִזְרָ֔ע וְכַרְמְךָ֖ לֹ֥א תִזְמֹֽר׃

But in the seventh year the land shall have a sabbath of complete rest, a sabbath of God: you shall not sow your field or prune your vineyard.

אֵ֣ת סְפִ֤יחַ קְצִֽירְךָ֙ לֹ֣א תִקְצ֔וֹר וְאֶת־עִנְּבֵ֥י נְזִירֶ֖ךָ לֹ֣א תִבְצֹ֑ר שְׁנַ֥ת שַׁבָּת֖וֹן יִהְיֶ֥ה לָאָֽרֶץ׃

You shall not reap the aftergrowth of your harvest or gather the grapes of your untrimmed vines; it shall be a year of complete rest for the land.[57]

These larger blocks of time carry a clear message imposing limits on human power. Every seventh year brings a "release" of a person's lands. No one is to plant or harvest. The sabbatical year is a Sabbath for the land itself with farmers surrendering all signs of mastery. In addition to abstaining from working the land, the book of Deuteronomy adds the precept that interpersonal debts are cancelled each seventh year so that each person

---

57 Leviticus 25:3-5

relinquishes power over another as well.[58]

The crescendo rises even further after seven cycles of seven years:

וְקִדַּשְׁתֶּם אֵת שְׁנַת הַחֲמִשִּׁים שָׁנָה וּקְרָאתֶם דְּרוֹר בָּאָרֶץ לְכָל־יֹשְׁבֶיהָ יוֹבֵל הִוא תִּהְיֶה לָכֶם וְשַׁבְתֶּם אִישׁ אֶל־אֲחֻזָּתוֹ וְאִישׁ אֶל־מִשְׁפַּחְתּוֹ תָּשֻׁבוּ:

and you shall hallow the fiftieth year. You shall proclaim release throughout the land for all its inhabitants. It shall be a jubilee for you: each of you shall return to your holding and each of you shall return to your family.[59]
During this fiftieth year, the Jubilee, still another period of ceasing to work the land is declared. Further, every form of behaving as master is erased. Slaves are released whether they wish to be freed or not, and lands purchased over the intervening years are returned to their original tribal owners. It is a time of radical social policy to teach a basic value:

וְהָאָרֶץ לֹא תִמָּכֵר לִצְמִתֻת כִּי־לִי הָאָרֶץ כִּי־גֵרִים וְתוֹשָׁבִים אַתֶּם עִמָּדִי:

But the land must not be sold beyond reclaim, for the land is Mine; you are but aliens resident with Me.[60]
The essential point is that God is the owner, and God's ownership never expires! A human being can never have a lasting title to the land. The text underscores this teaching by ascribing to the Jewish people the status of resident-aliens, גֵרִים וְתוֹשָׁבִים. This phrase is used in other contexts to refer to those who are living on the margins of society. Even in **the land** which was promised to them as a home, the Jewish people are tagged with this marginal status.

We do not know if or how this economic/social policy was ever fully implemented. Nonetheless, the legislation itself carries a seminal value reminding the Jewish people and humanity of the limits of their status. It seems natural to assume that one can become an owner. Property is bought

58 Deuteronomy 15:1-2
59 Leviticus 25:10
60 Leviticus 25:23

and sold in probably every culture. Title is enshrined in law and can be passed from one generation to the next. Documents or titles to ownership abound. This Torah legislation challenges these ingrained assumptions and asks how it is that human beings ever had the right to ownership of something that ultimately could not be "owned". The words "the land is Mine; you are but aliens resident with Me." is counter-cultural. God the Creator is the Owner. The human family is regarded as stewards. The earth is never given over to human ownership. Should one forget, each Sabbath, each Sabbatical Year, and each Jubilee comes to rein in our hubris.

There are many Names for God in Jewish tradition. One that is enshrined in daily prayers is: קונה הכל, the Possessor, the Owner of all. It is not among the most frequently used Names, but this Name seems to speak to this moment. This Name has pride of place liturgically, found as it is in the opening paragraph of the Amidah, the culminating prayer in daily worship. It is a Name that is invoked at least three times a day without fail each day of the year.

In modern life, we are accustomed to ownership. We live in a consumer centered society in which there is so much to acquire, to own. Even as children, we quickly learn that some precious toys can belong to us, and we will struggle to assert our ownership if a sibling or friend competes for their use. We grow into consuming adults where a car, a business, and a home can become "ours". With larger acquisitions, there is paperwork, a title, to be carefully preserved. We buy and sell naturally and frequently.

When we constitute ourselves as nations, we collectively claim that we "own" the land within our country's boundaries. We "own" the rights to extract useful minerals from the earth. We "own" fishing rights in bodies of water within or adjacent to our boundaries. Even the atmosphere above us is "our" airspace. We tend not to question these proprietary claims.

Pushing back against our attachment to possessions and our assumption of ownership, this teaching of Torah attempts to loosen our hold on things of this world. If God is the Possessor, the Owner of all, our "possessions" are seen in a different light. It is not that we are forbidden to buy and sell; rather we are reminded that what we have is on loan, that we are guardians. What we acquire is not truly ours. What we have is handed to us on condition that we care for it well and hand it on unblemished to the next generation.

In a notable kabbalistic text, we are taught:

The wisdom that is essential for a person is (first and foremost) that one know how to delve into the secrets of one's Possessor (קונו).[61]
If our world and everything it contains, even the powers invested in our body and soul, are never "owned" by us, the implications are profound. What we have should be treasured as a loan, handled humbly, generously shared with others in need, always acknowledged with gratitude. It should be inconceivable to take for granted or to trash anything which is not truly our own.

This teaching "כי לי הארץ", "the earth is Mine" is visionary. Title to ownership is so deeply entrenched in modern societies that it is unlikely to be altered. However, this concept serves as a reminder that there is a deeper truth about Who really is entitled to act as an owner. It should give us cause to reconsider how ownership might be exercised with a lighter touch, with more compassion and more love.

---

61 Zohar Chadash, "Midrash Shir HaShirim", 18a-18b

CHAPTER FOUR

NUMBERS

Humility

Moses, ancient Israel's great leader, is praised for one quality, his humility:

וְהָאִישׁ מֹשֶׁה עָנָו מְאֹד מִכֹּל הָאָדָם אֲשֶׁר עַל־פְּנֵי הָאֲדָמָה׃

Now Moses himself was very humble, more so than any other human being on earth.[62]

He never sought the power that was bestowed on him. In fact, he steadfastly turned away from God's offer of leadership until finally relenting. When others in the encampment, Eldad and Medad, began to prophesize, seemingly challenging his unique link to God, he responded to those who wished to silence these new prophets:

וַיֹּאמֶר לוֹ מֹשֶׁה הַמְקַנֵּא אַתָּה לִי וּמִי יִתֵּן כָּל־עַם יְהֹוָה נְבִיאִים כִּי־יִתֵּן יְהֹוָה אֶת־רוּחוֹ עֲלֵיהֶם׃

But Moses said to him, "Are you wrought up on my account? Would that all God's people were prophets, that God put [the divine] spirit upon them!"[63]

Moses dreamed of all the people sharing in the gift of prophecy. When thereafter it was time to pass on the mantel of leadership to Joshua, there was no sense of rancor for Moses. The transition of power was completely peaceful.

What is humility? Rabbi Judah Loew, kabbalist and scholar in 16th Century Prague, answers:

The quality of humility exists when a person does not attribute to oneself a unique level which then separates one from other people. Rather one is equal to all, and this is peace. For disagreement emerges when everyone

---

62 Numbers 12:3
63 Numbers 11:29

49

sees oneself as being on a higher level, and thus argument breaks out. Yet a humble person has no part in argument.[64]

Humility before God and others becomes a central theme in Jewish ethics, but it is also linked to the wonders of nature.

כִּי־אֶרְאֶה שָׁמֶיךָ מַעֲשֵׂה אֶצְבְּעֹתֶיךָ יָרֵחַ וְכוֹכָבִים אֲשֶׁר כּוֹנָנְתָּה:

When I behold Your heavens, the work of Your fingers,
the moon and stars that You set in place,

מָה־אֱנוֹשׁ כִּי־תִזְכְּרֶנּוּ וּבֶן־אָדָם כִּי תִפְקְדֶנּוּ:

what is man that You have been mindful of him,
mortal man that You have taken note of him.[65]

In the midrash when the first human beings display some degree of vanity at their place at the pinnacle of the creation narrative, they are rudely put in their place in the words of the midrash:

אמר אדם משברא הקדוש ברוך הוא כל בהמה והעופות והשקצים והרמשים אחר כך ברא אותי ומפני מה שאם יגבה לבו עליו, אומרים לו ומפני מה יגבה לבך עליך, יתוש וזבוב אחד קדמך לבריאה

Adam said: When the Holy One created every animal, birds, and creeping creatures, afterwards God created me! Why (this order)? Should the human being's heart become prideful, they say to him: "Why should your heart be prideful? The mosquito and the fly preceded you in creation!"[66]

The earth, the water, the plant and animal kingdoms all came into existence and thrived before the appearance of human beings.

Aldo Leopold echoes this demand for humility in the face of the complexity of the ecosystem:

He (the scientist) knows that the biotic mechanism is so complex that

---

64 Maharal of Prague, Netivot Shalom 1, "The Pathway of Peace", Chapter 1
65 Psalms 8:4-5
66 Midrash Aggadah (Buber), Leviticus, "Tazria" 12:2

its workings may never be completely understood.[67]
The advancement of knowledge only adds to wonder at the intricacy of the
web of interdependence in which we are embedded.

With even a little bit of knowledge and with much power, human
beings are very susceptible to hubris. In our age, humanity wields ever
greater power along with a growing body of knowledge, making arrogance
even more likely. Moses stood as close as possible to the Source of All. He
was the greatest leader of the Jewish people. Yet, he remained at his core a
very humble man. He stands as a compelling model of how power can be
joined with undiminished humility.

The Earth Swallows the Guilty

As we have seen in earlier passages, the earth is an active respondent
to human activity, especially to human failings. The earth refuses to yield
its produce to transgressors; it exiles people from their homes due to serious
wrongdoing. It "vomits" out those guilty of violation of basic commandments. Korach, a member of the priestly tribe of Levi, led a rebellion against
the power of Moses and Aaron. In the narrative describing the fate of Korach,
the earth is once again a key actor:

וְאִם־בְּרִיאָ֞ה יִבְרָ֣א יְהֹוָ֗ה וּפָצְתָ֨ה הָאֲדָמָ֤ה אֶת־פִּ֙יהָ֙ וּבָלְעָ֤ה אֹתָם֙ וְאֶת־כׇּל־אֲשֶׁ֣ר לָהֶ֔ם וְיָרְד֥וּ חַיִּ֖ים שְׁאֹ֑לָה
וִֽידַעְתֶּ֕ם כִּ֧י נִֽאֲצ֛וּ הָאֲנָשִׁ֥ים הָאֵ֖לֶּה אֶת־יְהֹוָֽה׃

*But if God brings about something unheard-of, so that the ground opens its
mouth and swallows them up with all that belongs to them, and they go down
alive into Sheol, you shall know that those involved have spurned God."*

וַיְהִי֙ כְּכַלֹּת֔וֹ לְדַבֵּ֕ר אֵ֥ת כׇּל־הַדְּבָרִ֖ים הָאֵ֑לֶּה וַתִּבָּקַע֙ הָֽאֲדָמָ֔ה אֲשֶׁ֖ר תַּחְתֵּיהֶֽם׃

*Scarcely had he finished speaking all these words when the ground under
them burst asunder,*

---

67 Op Cit., Leopold, Aldo, p. 173

וַתִּפְתַּ֨ח הָאָ֜רֶץ אֶת־פִּ֗יהָ וַתִּבְלַ֤ע אֹתָם֙ וְאֶת־בָּתֵּיהֶ֔ם וְאֵ֤ת כָּל־הָֽאָדָם֙ אֲשֶׁ֣ר לְקֹ֔רַח וְאֵ֖ת כָּל־הָֽרְכֽוּשׁ׃

and the earth opened its mouth and swallowed them up with their households, all Korach's people and all their possessions.[68]

Instead of vomiting the rebels out, here the earth swallows the rebels, sending them to their end in an unspecified place of oblivion. The Earth is not a bystander to human activity on its surface.

---

68 Numbers 16:30-32

52

CHAPTER FIVE

DEUTERONOMY

The fifth book of the Torah, **Deuteronomy,** while revisiting many details of law that are found in earlier books, is rich in new commandments which relate to reverence for the Earth and its unnumbered species.

The Blessing: Framing the Act of Eating

וְאָכַלְתָּ וְשָׂבָעְתָּ וּבֵרַכְתָּ אֶת־יְהוָה אֱלֹהֶיךָ עַל־הָאָרֶץ הַטֹּבָה אֲשֶׁר נָתַן־לָךְ:

When you have eaten your fill, give thanks to your God for the good land given to you.[69]

This single verse from **Deuteronomy** provides the opening for a vast outpouring of creativity in the evolution of Jewish liturgy. The "blessing" in Jewish practice stems from this simple commandment to express gratitude for the food we eat. It became a paradigm. The idea of saying aloud blessings was applied to every sphere of human pleasure. These well-chosen words assert that mundane, everyday activities can be the occasion for an intimate encounter with the Divine and an opportunity for thanksgiving. Each blessing tersely and directly names the reason for the blessing. The sages extended the reach of blessings from food and drink to other rich sources of enjoyment in sight, in hearing, in smell, and in touch. The "b'rachah", blessing, is a primary reminder of the need for gratitude and wonder at the daily gifts provided on Earth. Ideally no everyday source of pleasure should be taken for granted. A vital, daily sense of wonder leads to gratitude in the view of the rabbis; and the consequence of both should be vigilance in caring for this Earth, the abundant source of wonder.

---

69 Deuteronomy 8:10

The Second Paragraph of the SHMA

The three passages of Torah which constitute the heart of the Shema, the quintessential expression of Jewish faith, are central to Jewish liturgy. There is no day in the calendar on which they are omitted, accompanying a traditionally observant Jew morning and evening without fail. Often, these words are committed to memory. The sages of the Mishnah surely considered the ideas they contain to be pivotal.

Yet the second passage of the Shema has proved to be problematic for many. It seems to assert a reality which often does not square with human experience:

וְהָיָה אִם־שָׁמֹעַ תִּשְׁמְעוּ אֶל־מִצְוֹתַי אֲשֶׁר אָנֹכִי מְצַוֶּה אֶתְכֶם הַיּוֹם לְאַהֲבָה אֶת־יְהוָה אֱלֹהֵיכֶם וּלְעָבְדוֹ בְּכָל־לְבַבְכֶם וּבְכָל־נַפְשְׁכֶם:

If, then, you obey the commandments that I enjoin upon you this day, loving your God and serving [God] with all your heart and soul,

וְנָתַתִּי מְטַר־אַרְצְכֶם בְּעִתּוֹ יוֹרֶה וּמַלְקוֹשׁ וְאָסַפְתָּ דְגָנֶךָ וְתִירֹשְׁךָ וְיִצְהָרֶךָ:

I will grant the rain for your land in season, the early rain and the late. You shall gather in your new grain and wine and oil –

וְנָתַתִּי עֵשֶׂב בְּשָׂדְךָ לִבְהֶמְתֶּךָ וְאָכַלְתָּ וְשָׂבָעְתָּ:

I will also provide grass in the fields for your cattle – and thus you shall eat your fill.

הִשָּׁמְרוּ לָכֶם פֶּן יִפְתֶּה לְבַבְכֶם וְסַרְתֶּם וַעֲבַדְתֶּם אֱלֹהִים אֲחֵרִים וְהִשְׁתַּחֲוִיתֶם לָהֶם:

Take care not to be lured away to serve other gods and bow to them.

וְחָרָה אַף־יְהוָה בָּכֶם וְעָצַר אֶת־הַשָּׁמַיִם וְלֹא־יִהְיֶה מָטָר וְהָאֲדָמָה לֹא תִתֵּן אֶת־יְבוּלָהּ וַאֲבַדְתֶּם מְהֵרָה מֵעַל הָאָרֶץ הַטֹּבָה אֲשֶׁר יְהוָה נֹתֵן לָכֶם:

For God's anger will flare up against you, shutting up the skies so that there will be no rain and the ground will not yield its produce; and you will soon perish from the good land that God is assigning to you.[70]

Reward and punishment emanating from nature because of human moral achievement or failure simply do not seem obvious. As a result, some editors in the publication of modern books of prayer omitted these verses entirely. Others committed to the traditional text quietly question the literal validity of these ideas which are prominent in other locations in the book of **Deuteronomy** as well.

The modern climate crisis has brought these same words into startling relevance once more. We know that human action has assaulted the world around us in so many ways. Rain forests have been decimated. Pollution has degraded waterways and air quality. Plastic waste insinuates itself into virtually every corner of the earth even far from human habitation and collects shamefully in uncounted tons of debris where currents converge in the Pacific Ocean. Precious species have been decimated to the point of extinction. And heat retaining gases primarily from extracting and burning fossil fuels continue to rise in our atmosphere to unprecedented levels.

The human family has disregarded its responsibilities to care for the Earth itself. Now it has become very clear that there are consequences emanating from the Earth and its atmosphere. The Earth can only take so much abuse. Extremes in weather patterns, scorching heat, wildfires, drought, and flooding reach new records with almost every passing day. Will the Earth become uninhabitable due to human transgression?

As discussed earlier, the Torah posits that a very broad band of human moral action is reflected and registered in the Earth. The close relationship of human behavior to the Earth's functioning broadly is generally very subtle even to the point of being undetectable. In compelling contrast, when misbehavior is directed towards the world itself, there is a new clarity about action and reaction. We clearly cannot degrade this Earth without dire results.

---

70 Deuteronomy 11:13-17

Now the second paragraph of the Shema stands out in **bold** as a daily reminder that our excesses vis a vis the earth yield palpable consequences:

וְלֹא־יִהְיֶ֣ה מָטָ֗ר וְהָ֣אֲדָמָ֔ה לֹ֥א תִתֵּ֖ן אֶת־יְבוּלָ֑הּ וַאֲבַדְתֶּ֣ם מְהֵרָ֗ה מֵעַל֙ הָאָ֣רֶץ הַטֹּבָ֔ה אֲשֶׁ֥ר יְהֹוָ֖ה נֹתֵ֥ן לָכֶֽם׃

There will be no rain and the ground will not yield its produce; and you will soon perish from the good land that God is assigning to you.[71]

That the danger inherent in abusive human power could even cause a decisive rift between humanity and the ground on which we stand was recognized millennia ago in Torah. Strong language like "perish" is employed. The need to restore harmony between the earth and its human inhabitants before reaching the point of perishing becomes more urgent with each passing day.

The Power of One

In facing the climate crisis, a recurring response of the individual is one's feeling of powerlessness. How can an individual make a difference in the face of a global issue? The Torah's view is never to underestimate the power of each person:

רְאֵ֗ה אָנֹכִ֛י נֹתֵ֥ן לִפְנֵיכֶ֖ם הַיּ֑וֹם בְּרָכָ֖ה וּקְלָלָֽה׃

See, this day I set before you blessing and curse.[72]

The verse addresses every individual. Noticing an apparent inconsistency in grammar from singular to plural in this verse, the Kli Yakar comments:

ראה אנכי נותן לפניכם היום ברכה וקללה. ראה כמדבר ליחיד לפניכם כמדבר לרבים לפי שאמרו רז"ל לעולם ידמה לאדם כאילו היה כל העולם מחצה על מחצה זכויות ועונות עשה מצוה אחת הכריע את עצמו ואת כל העולם לכף זכות לכך אמר אל כל יחיד ראה שיראה בעין שכלו כי כל מעשיו יחזרו לפניכם לכולכם, והזכיר ענין זה בפרשה זו המדברת מענין הר גריזים והר עיבל כי שם נעשו כל ישראל ערבים זה בעד זה ומצד הערבות רבים נתפסים בעון היחיד.

See, this day I set before you blessing and curse: *"See" is as though addressed to an individual; "before you" is as though addressed to a multitude.*

---

71 Deuteronomy 11:17
72 Deuteronomy 11:26

This is in accord with what (the sages) said (Kedushin 40): 'A person should see oneself as though the whole world is balanced between merits and sins. If one does one mitzvah, one pushes the balance for oneself and for the entire world to the side of merit.' Thus, it is said to every person that one should see oneself that all of one's deeds will come "before you (plural)", to all of you. And this matter is mentioned in this Torah portion which speaks of the events at Mt. Gerizim and Mt. Eval, for it was there that all of Israel became responsible for one another; and due to this responsibility, the multitude is affected by the sin of the individual.[73]

We can never know the possible effects of our deeds, how a very personal decision can send currents out joining with the efforts of others. Perhaps, the rabbis speculate, what we do in any moment, added to the deeds of countless others, might create the critical mass which changes everything.[74] Even in a time when more than eight billion people live on the planet, the power of one cannot be overestimated.

Giving the First of the Harvest and the Firstborn of the Herd

וַהֲבֵאתֶ֣ם שָׁ֗מָּה עֹלֹ֤תֵיכֶם֙ וְזִבְחֵיכֶ֔ם וְאֵת֙ מַעְשְׂרֹ֣תֵיכֶ֔ם וְאֵ֖ת תְּרוּמַ֣ת יֶדְכֶ֑ם וְנִדְרֵיכֶם֙ וְנִדְבֹ֣תֵיכֶ֔ם וּבְכֹרֹ֖ת בְּקַרְכֶ֥ם וְצֹאנְכֶֽם׃

And there you are to bring your burnt offerings and other sacrifices, your tithes and contributions, your votive and freewill offerings, and the firstlings of your herds and flocks.[75]

Deuteronomy is replete with admonishments that what we have belongs to God. Such willingness to relinquish our human power can be crucial to addressing the climate crisis. First let's look at some examples of this recurrent reminder.

---

73 Kli Yakar on Deuteronomy 11:26
74 Compare to Keyes, Jr., Kenneth, The Hundredth Monkey, (Coos Bay, Oregon: Vision Books,1983)
75 Deuteronomy 12:6

The weekly Torah reading entitled "Re-eh" describes the obligatory gifts that Jewish farmers or herders should set aside from their harvest or animals. Note that the required gifts were from the **first and the best** of crops or animals. The farmer or herder could not benefit from the harvest without first setting aside these gifts which would be delivered to the Central Sanctuary or consumed only there, provided to the priests, or given to the needy.

To surrender willingly the first and finest fruits for anyone who worked tirelessly in the fields or pastures could only be explained as a limit on the concept of ownership. These obligations were a constant reminder that everything ultimately belongs to God. Here is an echo of what we learned in earlier passages about ownership and how humans ultimately are only caretakers of what the land yields. The ability of the earth to yield fruit, the capacity of cattle to bear young, and the wisdom and strength of farmers and shepherds to care for their fields and herds were all made available by a Higher Source. Acknowledging the Source concretely by loosening one's grip on one's possessions became a constant motif in Torah.

Relinquishing Power

מִקֵּץ שֶׁבַע־שָׁנִים תַּעֲשֶׂה שְׁמִטָּה:

Every seventh year you shall practice remission of debts.

וְזֶה דְּבַר הַשְּׁמִטָּה שָׁמוֹט כָּל־בַּעַל מַשֵּׁה יָדֹו אֲשֶׁר יַשֶּׁה בְּרֵעֵהוּ לֹא־יִגֹּשׂ אֶת־רֵעֵהוּ וְאֶת־אָחִיו כִּי־קָרָא שְׁמִטָּה לַיהוָה:

This shall be the nature of the remission: all creditors shall remit the due that they claim from their fellow [Israelites]; they shall not dun their fellow [Israelites] or kin, for the remission proclaimed is of God.[76]

כִּי־יִמָּכֵר לְךָ אָחִיךָ הָעִבְרִי אֹו הָעִבְרִיָּה וַעֲבָדְךָ שֵׁשׁ שָׁנִים וּבַשָּׁנָה הַשְּׁבִיעִת תְּשַׁלְּחֶנּוּ חָפְשִׁי מֵעִמָּךְ:

---

76 Deuteronomy 15:1-2

If a fellow Hebrew man – or woman – is sold to you, he shall serve you six years, and in the seventh year you shall set him free.[77]

Adding to the limits imposed in the Sabbatical Year described in the book of **Leviticus**, the Torah now adds two new boundaries on human power. Every creditor had to cancel every debtor's obligation. Any debt accrued had a time limit, every seventh year. And if a fellow Jew became an indentured servant, freedom was granted unconditionally in that same seventh year. In the world of the Biblical writer, holding others as slaves was still an accepted institution. Arguably enslaving another human being is the most egregious exercise of power. Even in antiquity in the Biblical view, there was to be a time of release. Acting as a creditor or controlling the very life of another human being were expressions of power of one over another. Added to the obligation to leave one's land untilled, mastery in any form was periodically denied.

Giving According to God's Gifts

אִישׁ כְּמַתְּנַת יָדוֹ כְּבִרְכַּת יְהוָה אֱלֹהֶיךָ אֲשֶׁר נָתַן־לָךְ׃

Each person with his own gift in accordance with the blessing that God has given you.[78]

From a grammatical detail in the text, the Kli Yakar teaches once more that all that a person owns has its source in God.

א"כ היל"ל כמתנת ידך, ואמר ידו בלשון נסתר ואולי **,שבכל הפרשה משה ידבר בנוכח לישראל** כי ממך הכל ומידך נתנו לך. ואמר לשון זה בעולות שכולם (ד"ה א' כט יד)קאי ידו על הקב"ה כמ"ש כליל לגבוה פן ירע עיניו מליתן משלו לגבוה כל כך עולות הרבה, ע"כ אמר שלא משלו הוא נותן אלא ממה שקבל מידו של הקב"ה וז"ש כמתנת ידו של הקב"ה אם יתן לו נכסים מרובים אז יחזור ויתן לו משלו ויביא עולות מרובים

In the entire Torah portion, Moses speaks in second person to Israel. If

---

so, the text should have said: "each with your own gift". (Instead) it says "his gift" impersonally. Perhaps (it means) from God's hand as it is said: "everything comes from You. And from Your hand, God gives it to you." And this text refers to the "olot" offerings which were completely consumed (as a sacrifice) to God lest one feel reluctance giving so much of one's own gift to God. Therefore, it is said that one is giving not from one's own but rather from that which one received from the Divine hand. Thus, it says to give in accordance with "His gift". If one's multitude of possessions are given from the Divine hand, then one should return them (which came from) God and bring many offerings.[79]

We have seen a drumbeat across many passages in Torah teaching that nothing really belongs to a human being. Land, animals, debts owed by others, and, in the ancient world, even indentured servants or slaves are, one by one, not subject to human ownership. The repetition may point to a recognition that there is a strong tendency to assume ownership in human affairs. To strip humanity of ownership goes against the grain. Especially with hard work, humans assume that they can accumulate possessions. Again and again, that assumption of ownership is denied.

The implications of living in a world without personal possessions are critical in this time of climate crisis. If everything in one's tenure on earth is on loan, a person should treat everything in one's domain with care. Nothing that belongs to Another can be despoiled. Instead, we are directed to tread softly and with humility so that at least we are not the cause of degradation.

In these many ways, Torah legislation continually reminds a Jew that the power bestowed on a human being is severely limited. Power is an undeniable gift. Yet wherever we turn, we encounter boundaries and signs that our power is not absolute. By relinquishing it entirely from time to time and bumping into limits on its exercise, we learn to wield power with compassion and to be ready to surrender it entirely when the need arises.

79 Kli Yakar on Deuteronomy 16:17

A King Must Never be a Master

In another of the weekly Torah readings, "Shoftim", the coronation of a king included a description of limitations on the king's power. He must personally write a Torah scroll and carry it with him so that he is guided by the Torah's values. His treasury is limited, symbolized by his not having a large corral of horses. Surprisingly, he is instructed not to send his people back to Egypt:

רַק לֹא־יַרְבֶּה־לּוֹ סוּסִים וְלֹא־יָשִׁיב אֶת־הָעָם מִצְרַיְמָה לְמַעַן הַרְבּוֹת סוּס וַיהוָה אָמַר לָכֶם לֹא תֹסִפוּן לָשׁוּב בַּדֶּרֶךְ הַזֶּה עוֹד:

Moreover, he shall not keep many horses or send people back to Egypt to add to his horses, since God has warned you, "You must not go back that way again."[80]

Why would anyone think of sending his people back to Egypt? Rabbi Aaron Samuel Tamares, a unique rabbinic voice in the early 20th Century in Eastern Europe, suggests:

כל הפרשה ההיא הנה באה להטיף לקח נשגב במשפט המלוכה הישראלית, שעל מלך ישראל הוטל לבל ישים מבטחו לא ברבוי הכסף והזהב ולא ברבוי הסוסים הדוהרים פן ,,ישיב את העם..מצרימה", כלומר אל מנהגי המצרים העריצים ,, וה' אמר", כלומר במפולו שנטפל הוא בעצמו בנקמת מצרים ולא נתן לישראל להשתתף במעשה הנקמה הרי הוא כאילו אמר להם והזהירם: ,,לא תוסיפון לשוב בדרך הזה (דרך המצרים הבוטחים בכח אגרופם) עוד.

All of this section comes to bestow an elevated teaching for the laws of Israelite kingship. For it is incumbent upon a king of Israel not to place his trust either in an abundance of silver and gold or in an abundance of galloping horses lest he "cause the people to return to Egypt," meaning (to return to) the tyrannical ways of the Egyptians,"and [is it not] as the Lord has said to you," i.e., in His engagement (in the Exodus) in which He Himself took revenge against Egypt and did not permit Israel to take part at all in the acts of revenge, it was as though He warned them: "Do not ever

---

80 Deuteronomy 17:16

return to this way (the way of the Egyptians who trust in the power of the fist) again."[81]

In the view of Rabbi Tamares, returning to Egypt would symbolize the worst abuse of power. As we have seen, other mitzvot offered guardrails so that power was to be relinquished over land and over possessions; but the most egregious abuse would be to enslave other people as the Egyptians had done. God is frequently identified as the liberator from enslavement in Egypt. God was modeling for the Jewish people. The takeaway for the Jewish future was to abhor such abuse of power and to resolve never to lord it over others. Much of the message in Torah guards those limits of power.

Bal Tashchit: No Wanton Destruction

How should one treat anything that one is given in this life? The guidance from Torah stems from an unlikely source:

כִּי־תָצוּר אֶל־עִיר יָמִים רַבִּים לְהִלָּחֵם עָלֶיהָ לְתָפְשָׂהּ לֹא־תַשְׁחִית אֶת־עֵצָהּ לִנְדֹּחַ עָלָיו גַּרְזֶן כִּי מִמֶּנּוּ תֹאכֵל וְאֹתוֹ לֹא תִכְרֹת כִּי הָאָדָם עֵץ הַשָּׂדֶה לָבֹא מִפָּנֶיךָ בַּמָּצוֹר:

When in your war against a city you have to besiege it a long time in order to capture it, you must not destroy its trees, wielding the ax against them. You may eat of them, but you must not cut them down. Are trees of the field human to withdraw before you into the besieged city?[82]

The immediate context relates to the rules of engagement when besieging a city in war. The besieging army should not destroy fruit-bearing trees. The plain sense of this rule of war making is to preserve these trees for the benefit of one's own army as a source of nourishment.

From this very limited precept, the sages developed a far-reaching mitzvah not to lay waste or to ruin anything with which one is blessed. Maimonides speaks to the vast extension of this precept:

---

81 Tamares, Rabbi Aaron Samuel, Mussar HaTorah v'Hayahadut, "Liberty", (Vilna: S.P. Garber, 1912)
82 Deuteronomy 20:19

וְלֹא הָאִילָנוֹת בִּלְבַד. אֶלָּא כָּל הַמְשַׁבֵּר כֵּלִים. וְקוֹרֵעַ בְּגָדִים. וְהוֹרֵס בִּנְיָן. וְסוֹתֵם מַעְיָן. וּמְאַבֵּד מַאֲכָלוֹת
דֶּרֶךְ הַשְׁחָתָה. עוֹבֵר בְּלֹא תַשְׁחִית. וְאֵינוֹ לוֹקֶה אֶלָּא מַכַּת מַרְדּוּת מִדִּבְרֵיהֶם:

*This prohibition does not apply to trees alone. Rather, anyone who breaks
utensils, tears garments, destroys buildings, stops up a spring, or ruins food
with a destructive intent transgresses the command 'Do not destroy.'*[83]

Moshe Cordovero, scholar and mystic of the 16th Century, teaches
extreme care for all creatures and all of one's possessions:

ולא יבזה שום נמצא ולא יעקור צמח אלא לצורך ולא ימית בעל חי אלא לצורך ויברור להם מיתה יפה
כל מה דאפשר.

*One should not despise anything that exists and not uproot anything that
grows except for one's needs and not kill any animal except for one's needs
and one should choose a compassionate death (for the animal) as much as
possible.*[84]

Rabbi Samson Raphael Hirsch eloquently summarizes the vast
application of this Torah law:

*The prohibition of "destroying trees" without purpose at the time
of laying siege is given only as an example, and "bal tashchit", "do not
destroy" is a prohibition against destroying anything wantonly. Thus "bal
tashchit" said here is a sweeping warning to humanity: Do not abuse your
status in the world to destroy things due to one's mood, desire, or even
without thinking. God placed God's world before humanity to use it wisely.
Only for this purpose did God give one the power to "conquer" the land and
to "have dominion" over it.*[85]

Returning to the context in Torah concerning fruit bearing trees, Bal
Tashchit retains a special affinity to food waste today. It is estimated that

---

83 Maimonides, Mishneh Torah, "Hilchot M'lachim", Chapter 6, Halachah 10
84 Cordovero, Moshe, Tomer Devorah, Chapter 3
85 Hirsch, Rabbi Samson Raphael, Commentary on Torah, Deuteronomy 20:20

31% of emissions globally result from the food supply.[86] From household management to grocery chains to restaurants and beyond, there is an urgent need to correct this shameful source of waste especially while so many go hungry.

The concept of "Bal Tashchit" "Do not wantonly destroy" is taken from its limited context in war and applied with broad strokes to the treatment of anything one owns and any encounter with the world at large. It is a vivid example of "a mountain hanging from a hair", a value with sparse biblical roots but with many, sprawling precepts in Jewish law. Clearly, the sages over time were very eager to build out this idea of treating everything in this world with respect. We should not lead a wasteful life.

The text adds an intriguing detail "כִּי הָאָדָם עֵץ הַשָּׂדֶה", "a person is a tree of the field". In context, these words can be read as a question as it is in the translation above. But it can also be understood as a declarative phrase. Some commentators find in these words a rich metaphor of what it can mean to be human. Like a tree, a person can grow, mature, reproduce not only with progeny but with good works. Just as a tree offers so many benefits with its shade, its provision of safety and housing for many other creatures in addition to its fruit, likewise a human being can emulate these qualities in the way that he or she chooses to live. The Torah itself is a "Tree of Life". The Menorah in the desert sanctuary and in the Temple in Jerusalem was formed suggesting the image of a fruit bearing tree. The image of a tree became deeply ingrained in Jewish symbols and liturgy, underlining our connection to these remarkable living things with which we share the earth.

Sustaining Species

To nourish ourselves, the Torah clearly permits taking the lives of other beings who swim in the sea or live on land. There are limits imposed

---

86 https://www.carbonbrief.org/food-waste-makes-up-half-of-global-food-system-emissions/

by Kashrut. However, there are rich choices of animals that can be used for food. The eggs of kosher birds are permitted. In the Torah portion entitled "Ki Teitzei", the provision regarding a bird's nest can be found:

כִּי יִקָּרֵא קַן־צִפּוֹר ׀ לְפָנֶיךָ בַּדֶּרֶךְ בְּכָל־עֵץ ׀ אוֹ עַל־הָאָרֶץ אֶפְרֹחִים אוֹ בֵיצִים וְהָאֵם רֹבֶצֶת עַל־הָאֶפְרֹחִים אוֹ עַל־הַבֵּיצִים לֹא־תִקַּח הָאֵם עַל־הַבָּנִים:

If, along the road, you chance upon a bird's nest, in any tree or on the ground, with fledglings or eggs and the mother sitting over the fledglings or on the eggs, do not take the mother together with her young.[87]

Commenting on this verse, the Ramban explains:

כי יקרא קן צפור לפניך גם זו מצוה מבוארת מן אותו ואת בנו לא תשחטו ביום אחד (ויקרא כב כח) כי הטעם בשניהם לבלתי היות לנו לב אכזרי ולא נרחם או שלא יתיר הכתוב לעשות השחתה לעקור המין אע"פ שהתיר השחיטה במין ההוא והנה ההורג האם והבנים ביום אחד או לוקח אותם בהיות להם דרור לעוף כאלו יכרית המין ההוא

IF A BIRD'S NEST HAPPENS TO BE BEFORE YOU. This also is an explanatory commandment, of the prohibition ye shall not kill it (the mother) and its young both in one day, because the reason for both [commandments] is that we should not have a cruel heart and be discompassionate, or it may be that Scripture does not permit us to destroy a species altogether, although it permits slaughter [for food] within that group. Now, he who kills the dam and the young in one day or takes them when they are free to fly [it is regarded] as though he cut off that species.[88]

It is the way of the world that species sustain themselves by feeding on each other. According to Ramban, the purpose of sending away the mother bird is to assure that there may be more eggs and chicks in the future. Even in the act of searching for food, one should take steps to protect the sustainability of other species. Of course, there is self-interest involved in

---

87 Deuteronomy 22:6
88 Ramban on Deuteronomy 22:6

doing so, but the Ramban is making a deeper point that it is good to find a balance point so that species can continue to co-exist with us. Each species is precious apart from human need. The continuation of the narrative in Torah lends support to this value of sustainability:

שַׁלֵּחַ תְּשַׁלַּח אֶת־הָאֵם וְאֶת־הַבָּנִים תִּקַּח־לָךְ לְמַעַן יִיטַב לָךְ וְהַאֲרַכְתָּ יָמִים: {ס}

Let the mother go, and take only the young, in order that you may fare well and have a long life.[89]

The reward for performing this mitzvah is length of days. One's own life can be lengthened, but it comes hand in hand with the chance for other species to thrive as well. Caring for the continuing welfare of other species contributes to sustaining human life in the long term.

The Ramban connects the rationale for this commandment to the earlier precept that "ye shall not kill it [the mother] and its young both in one day." [90] He assumes that such a restriction is also understandable as a safeguard for the species of the mother who might subsequently bear more progeny.

A surprise connects the promised reward of longer life for the mitzvah regarding bird's nest to the fifth of the Ten Commandments to honor one's father and mother. Parallel language is used in each commandment.

כַּבֵּד אֶת־אָבִיךָ וְאֶת־אִמֶּךָ לְמַעַן יַאֲרִכוּן יָמֶיךָ עַל הָאֲדָמָה אֲשֶׁר־יְהוָה אֱלֹהֶיךָ נֹתֵן לָךְ: {ס}

Honor your father and your mother, that you may long endure on the land that your God is assigning to you.[91]

In general, Torah texts do not reveal the reward for fulfillment of a mitzvah. That the same promise is made for two such disparate commandments is unusual and attracts the attention of commentators. The most well-known speculation is that tying longer life to a fundamental teaching in the Ten Commandments and to a rather uncommon and marginal mitzvah teaches

---

89 Deuteronomy 22:7
90 Leviticus 22:28
91 Exodus 20:12

that one should not presume to know the relative weighing of any precept. Rather they should all be approached with equal devotion.

Another possible linkage is that both commandments deal with intergenerational relationships and the promise that they might continue to thrive into the future. The enterprise of Torah is intended to be long-term, reaching into the distant future. For such a future to be envisioned and approached, sustainability of life on earth for all species is vital.

It causes much pain to learn that the warming of this Earth by human agency could result in the extinction of a million species.[92] Saving a single human life is equivalent to saving a world. How can one calculate the loss forever of one million precious species?

Blessings and Curses

The second paragraph of the Shema cited above is the best-known assertion that humanity's and specifically the Jewish people's moral status would be the cause of natural prosperity or calamity. The more detailed account of how this would come to pass awaited the "tochechah", the reproach, found in the Torah portion "Ki Tavo". What is striking is that both reward and punishment are framed in terms of the effects of nature itself on human life. Blessings come first:

בָּרוּךְ אַתָּה בָּעִיר וּבָרוּךְ אַתָּה בַּשָּׂדֶה:

Blessed shall you be in the city and blessed shall you be in the country.

בָּרוּךְ פְּרִי־בִטְנְךָ וּפְרִי אַדְמָתְךָ וּפְרִי בְהֶמְתֶּךָ שְׁגַר אֲלָפֶיךָ וְעַשְׁתְּרוֹת צֹאנֶךָ:

Blessed shall be your issue from the womb, your produce from the soil, and the offspring of your cattle, the calving of your herd and the lambing of your flock.

---

92 https://www.ifaw.org/journal/animals-most-impacted-climate-change#:
~:text=How%20much%20is%20climate%20change,high%20risk%20of%20going%20extinct.

בָּרוּךְ טַנְאֲךָ וּמִשְׁאַרְתֶּךָ:

Blessed shall be your basket and your kneading bowl.

יִפְתַּח יְהֹוָה ׀ לְךָ אֶת־אוֹצָרוֹ הַטּוֹב אֶת־הַשָּׁמַיִם לָתֵת מְטַר־אַרְצְךָ בְּעִתּוֹ וּלְבָרֵךְ אֵת כָּל־מַעֲשֵׂה יָדֶךָ וְהִלְוִיתָ גוֹיִם רַבִּים וְאַתָּה לֹא תִלְוֶה:

God will open for you that bounteous store, the heavens, to provide rain for your land in season and to bless all your undertakings. You will be creditor to many nations, but debtor to none.[93]

Curses are offered in ever greater detail:

אָרוּר אַתָּה בָּעִיר וְאָרוּר אַתָּה בַּשָּׂדֶה:

Cursed shall you be in the city and cursed shall you be in the country.

אָרוּר טַנְאֲךָ וּמִשְׁאַרְתֶּךָ:

Cursed shall be your basket and your kneading bowl.

אָרוּר פְּרִי־בִטְנְךָ וּפְרִי אַדְמָתֶךָ שְׁגַר אֲלָפֶיךָ וְעַשְׁתְּרֹת צֹאנֶךָ:

Cursed shall be your issue from the womb and your produce from the soil, the calving of your herd and the lambing of your flock.

וְהָיוּ שָׁמֶיךָ אֲשֶׁר עַל־רֹאשְׁךָ נְחֹשֶׁת וְהָאָרֶץ אֲשֶׁר־תַּחְתֶּיךָ בַּרְזֶל:

The skies above your head shall be copper and the earth under you will be iron.

יִתֵּן יְהֹוָה אֶת־מְטַר אַרְצְךָ אָבָק וְעָפָר מִן־הַשָּׁמַיִם יֵרֵד עָלֶיךָ עַד הִשָּׁמְדָךְ:

God will make the rain of your land dust, and sand shall drop on you from the sky, until you are wiped out.

כְּרָמִים תִּטַּע וְעָבָדְתָּ וְיַיִן לֹא־תִשְׁתֶּה וְלֹא תֶאֱגֹר כִּי תֹאכְלֶנּוּ הַתֹּלָעַת:

Though you plant vineyards and till them, you shall have no wine to drink or store, for the worm shall devour them.

---

93 Deuteronomy 28:3-5,12

68

זֵיתִים יִהְיוּ לְךָ בְּכָל־גְּבוּלֶךָ וְשֶׁמֶן לֹא תָסוּךְ כִּי יִשַּׁל זֵיתֶךָ׃

*Though you have olive trees throughout your territory, you shall have no oil
for anointment, for your olives shall drop off.*

בָּנִים וּבָנוֹת תּוֹלִיד וְלֹא־יִהְיוּ לָךְ כִּי יֵלְכוּ בַּשֶּׁבִי׃

*Though you beget sons and daughters, they shall not remain with you, for
they shall go into captivity.*[94]

The effect of human action is not expressed in other-worldly terms.
It takes place here, in this world largely as natural events, either bringing
well-being or devastation. Homo sapiens and the earth share one fate. How
the human family functions determines the health of this large, intertwined
organism.

The news almost every day tells of events that seem taken directly
from these biblical passages. Scorching heat, drought, the failures of crops,
and so much more resemble the curses that were described thousands of
years ago. What is known with ever greater clarity is that they are the results
of an assault on the Earth, a failure of the human family to safeguard the
treasures that have been entrusted to all.

The Torah pictures an intricately interconnected ecosystem with
humanity at its apex. Long before modern science shed light on our linkage
to every species and to the health of the Earth itself, the Biblical writers
sensed that wondrous reality. Touching the world with care and with love
are essential for the welfare of the planet and for advancing forward the
drama of Jewish and world history.

---

94 Deuteronomy 28: 16-18,23-24,39-41

CHAPTER SIX

CONCLUSION

Summing Up

Emerging from the passages quoted above, six basic principles emerge:

Interdependence of Earth, all its Species and Humanity:
The sages recognized that the first man and woman were integrated into a single creative process that brought the earth, the heavens, and all terrestrial species into being. Humanity arose from the soil and returns to the soil like all other species. The closeness of this kinship is revealed in the Earth's response to human activity. Acting well towards one another and towards the Earth itself would bring prosperity and well-being. Sinfulness or any form of abuse result in rejection, even in exile. An assault on the Earth itself will surely not go unanswered.

The Unique Power of Human Being:
After appearing on the sixth day of the creation narrative in the Torah, the first human beings are immediately invested with power over the earth and its creatures. The arrival of the human species brings the ability to shape the environment.

Limits on Human Power:
While the power invested in humans is enormous and exceptional, the powers of body, mind, heart, and soul should be carefully constricted within limits. Human capacity is to be devoted to serving and guarding the Earth. Touching the Earth around us is inevitable, but it must be done with caring and with love.

Ownership Remains in God's Domain:
A human being never gains title to either the land or its produce. God, the Creator, is and remains the Owner. Periodically, especially on each Shabbat,

each Jew surrenders any pretensions of ownership. Instead, inhabitants are "resident aliens" wherever they dwell, even in the "Promised Land".

Humility:

Human power is to be joined with humility. Power and humility seem to be opposites, but Torah insists that they can and must be linked. The leadership of Moses stands as a dramatic example of how two such opposites can reside and function in a human life.

Hope:

Despite serious and continuing human errors, Torah never teaches despair. Built into creation itself is the possibility of re-creation. Built into every human life is the gift of atonement and the possibility of a new start as long as one lives. Collectively there is the potential with human creativity and compassion to heal this Earth.

A Long Horizon in Time

From the outset of the Jewish people's journey, destiny lay in a far distant and indeterminate future stretching to the horizons of time. Each generation is vital; but since no generation can complete the work of Tikkun Olam, perfecting the world, at least every one can aspire to be a strong link in the chain. Knowing the limits of one's own life and its connectedness to the past and to the future becomes crucial.

A classic Talmudic tale of Choni HaMe'aggel, Choni the "Circle-Maker" teaches the consequences of forgetting the need to plan for those who would follow:

יוֹמָא חַד הֲוָה אָזֵל בְּאוֹרְחָא, חַזְיֵיהּ לְהָהוּא גַּבְרָא דַּהֲוָה נָטַע חָרוּבָא, אֲמַר לֵיהּ: הַאי, עַד כַּמָּה שְׁנִין טָעֵין? אֲמַר לֵיהּ: עַד שִׁבְעִין שְׁנִין. אֲמַר לֵיהּ: פְּשִׁיטָא לָךְ דְּחָיֵית שִׁבְעִין שְׁנִין? אֲמַר לֵיהּ הַאי הַאי גַּבְרָא עָלְמָא בְּחָרוּבָא אַשְׁכַּחְתֵּיהּ. כִּי הֵיכִי דְּשָׁתְלוּ לִי אֲבָהָתַי שָׁתְלִי נָמֵי לִבְרָאי.

One day, he was walking along the road when he saw a certain man planting a carob tree. Choni said to him: This tree, after how many years

*will it **bear fruit**? The man **said to him:** It will not produce fruit **until seventy years** have passed. Choni **said to him: Is it obvious to you that you will live seventy years,** that you expect to benefit from this tree? **He said to him: That man** himself **found a world full of carob trees. Just as my ancestors planted for me, I too am planting for my descendants.**

יָתֵיב, קָא כָּרֵיךְ רִיפְתָּא, אֲתַאי לֵיהּ שִׁינְתָּא, נִים. אַהְדְּרָא לֵיהּ מְשׁוּנִּיתָא, אִיכַסִּי מֵעֵינָא, וְנִים שַׁבְעִין שְׁנִין. כִּי קָם, חַזְיֵיהּ לְהַהוּא גַּבְרָא דְּהוּא קָא מְלַקֵּט מִינַּיְיהוּ, אָמַר לֵיהּ: אַתְּ הוּא דִּשְׁתַלְתֵּיהּ? אָמַר לֵיהּ: בַּר בְּרֵיהּ אֲנָא. אָמַר לֵיהּ: שְׁמַע מִינַּהּ דִּנְיִימֵי שַׁבְעִין שְׁנִין. חֲזָא לַחֲמָר[תֵּ]יהּ דְּאָתְיְילִידָא לֵיהּ רַמְכֵי רַמְכֵי.

***Choni sat and ate bread. Sleep overcame him and he slept. A cliff formed around him, and he disappeared from sight and slept for seventy years. When he awoke, he saw a certain man gathering** carobs from that tree. **Choni said to him:** Are **you the one who planted** this tree? The man **said to him: I am his son's son. Choni said to him: I can learn from this that I have slept for seventy years,** and indeed **he saw that his donkey had sired several herds** during those many years.*

אֲזַל לְבֵיתֵיהּ אֲמַר לְהוּ: בְּרֵיהּ דְּחוֹנִי הַמְעַגֵּל מִי קַיָּים? אֲמַרוּ לֵיהּ: בְּרֵיהּ לֵיתָא, בַּר בְּרֵיהּ אִיתָא. אֲמַר לְהוּ: אֲנָא חוֹנִי הַמְעַגֵּל. לָא הֵימְנוּהוּ. אֲזַל לְבֵית הַמִּדְרָשׁ, שַׁמְעִינְהוּ לְרַבָּנַן דְּקָאָמְרִי: נְהִירָן שְׁמַעְתָּתִין כְּבִשְׁנֵי חוֹנִי הַמְעַגֵּל, דְּכִי הֲוֵי עָיֵיל לְבֵית מִדְרָשָׁא כֹּל קוּשְׁיָא דַּהֲווֹ לְהוּ לְרַבָּנַן הֲוָה מְפָרֵק לְהוּ. אָמַר לְהוּ: אֲנָא נִיהוּ, וְלָא הֵימְנוּהוּ, וְלָא עָבְדִי לֵיהּ יְקָרָא כִּדְמִבָּעֵי לֵיהּ. חֲלַשׁ דַּעְתֵּיהּ, בְּעָא רַחֲמֵי, וּמִית. אָמַר רָבָא: הַיְינוּ דְּאָמְרִי אִינָשֵׁי: אוֹ חַבְרוּתָא אוֹ מִיתוּתָא.

Choni went home and said to** the members of the household: **Is the son of Choni HaMe'aggel alive? They said to him: His son is no** longer with us, **but his son's son is** alive. **He said to them: I am Choni HaMe'aggel. They did not believe him. He went to the study hall,** where he **heard the Sages say** about one scholar: **His halakhot are as enlightening** and as clear **as in the years of Choni HaMe'aggel,** for when Choni HaMe'aggel **would enter the study hall he would resolve for the Sages any difficulty they had. Choni said to them: I am he,** but they did not believe him and did not pay **him proper respect. Choni became very upset, prayed for mercy, and died.

Rava said: This explains the folk saying *that people say: Either friendship or death,* as one who has no friends is better off dead.[95]

Choni was a hero in his day, but his momentary lapse in recognizing the needs of the next generation cost him much grief at the end of his life.

In contrast to Choni's skepticism about the future, Judaism tends to be hopeful. One fascinating detail embedded in the Hebrew language is the richness of hopeful terms describing the future. One liturgical example is found in the traditional prayer of thanksgiving after a full meal:

הָרַחֲמָן הוּא יִשְׁתַּבַּח לְדוֹר דּוֹרִים, וְיִתְפָּאַר בָּנוּ לָעַד וּלְנֵצַח נְצָחִים, וְיִתְהַדַּר בָּנוּ לָעַד וּלְעוֹלְמֵי עוֹלָמִים:

The Merciful One will be praised ***for all generations,*** *He will be glorified through us* ***forever*** *and* ***for all eternity;*** *and He will be honored through us* ***for time everlasting.***

The terms וּלְעוֹלְמֵי עוֹלָמִים, "for all generations" וּלְנֵצַח נְצָחִים, "forever and for all eternity" and וּלְעוֹלְמֵי עוֹלָמִים, "for time everlasting" are synonymous; and they are just a few expressions of an unending hope for and confidence in an abundant future. To assure such a future, it is necessary to guarantee a healthy planet on which Jewish history could unfold.

Embracing the Entire Biosphere

Rabbi Avraham Yitzchok Kook in the 20th Century, the first Ashkenazic Chief Rabbi in Palestine before the State of Israel was established, expands this idea of a long-term future to include more than Jewish needs. His "Fourfold Song" speaks to the need for an expanded human consciousness:

יש שהוא שר שירת נפשו, ובנפשו הוא מוצא את הכל, את מלא הסיפוק הרוחני במלואו.

ויש שהוא שר שירת האומה, יוצא הוא מתוך המעגל של נפשו הפרטית, שאינו מרוחבת כראוי ולא מיושבת ישוב אידיאלי, שואף למרומי עז, והוא מתדבק באהבה נעימה עם כללותה של כנסת ישראל, ועמה הוא שר שיריה, מצר בצרותיה, ומשתעשע בתקוותיה, הוגה דעות עליונות וטהורות על עברה ועל עתידה, וחוקר באהבה ובחכמת לב את תוכן רוחה הפנימית.

95 Talmud Taanit, 23a

ויש אשר עוד תתרחב נפשו עד שיוצא ומתפשט מעל גבול ישראל, לשיר את שירת האדם, רוחו הולך
ומתרחב בגאון כללות האדם והוד צלמו, שואף אל תעודתו הכללית ומצפה להשתלמותו העליונה,
וממקור חיים זה הוא שואב את כללות הגיונותיו ומחקריו, שאיפותיו וחזיונותיו.

ויש אשר עוד מזה למעלה ברוחב יתנשא, עד שמתאחד עם כל היקום כולו, עם כל הבריות, עם כל
העולמים, ועם כולם אומר שירה, זה הוא העוסק בפרק שירה בכל יום שמובטח לו שהוא בן העולם
הבא {מסכת ברכות יז ע"א}

ויש אשר עולה עם כל השירים הללו ביחד באגודה אחת, וכולם נותנים את קולותיהם, כולם יחד
מנעימים את זמריהם, וזה לתוך זה לשד וחיים, קול ששון וקול שמחה, קול צהלה וקול רנה, קול חדוה
וקול קדושה. שירת הנפש, שירת האומה, שירת האדם, שירת העולם, כולם יחד מתמזגות בקרבו בכל
עת ובכל שעה.

והתמימות הזאת במילואה עולה היא להיות שירת קודש, שירת אל, שירת ישראל, בעוצם עזה
ותפארתה, בעוצם אמתה וגדלה, ישראל שיר אל,שיר פשוט, שיר כפול, שיר משולש, שיר מרובע,
שיר השירים לשלומה, למלך שהשלום שלו.

*There is one who sings the **Song of Self.** And within one's self, finds everything; the full of one's spiritual satisfaction within one's own fullness.*

*And there is one who sings the **Song of Nation.** He steps out from the circle of his private concern, which he doesn't find sufficiently broad, nor idealistically grounding. He strives for fierce heights yet attaches himself with gentle love to the ensemble of Knesset Yisrael – the Jewish people, and with her sings her songs, shares in her distresses, delights in her hopes. Engrossed is he with thoughts elevated and pure regarding her past and future; with love and wise-heart, he studies her inner spiritual essence.*

*And there is one who broadens further her sense of self, until it extends and expands beyond the boundary of Israel, to sing the **Song of Humanity.** Her spirit advances and encompasses the majesty of humanity, the splendorous dignity of its divine image. She is drawn to common destiny and yearns for humanity's sublime self-actualization. From this life source she draws the principles of her ruminations and investigations, her ambitions and dreams. And there is one who still more expansively rises higher until one unifies one's self with all existence, with all creatures, and with all worlds. With* *all of them, one sings. This one engages one's self with Perek Shira – the daily **Song of World-Creation,** to whom it is forepromised that one will be worthy of the World-Yet-to-Come.*

And then there is one who arises with all these songs together in concert, all parts contributing their voices, all together harmonizing their melodies. One with another creating polyphonic vitality and life: They are the sounds of joy and jubilation, the sounds of rejoicing and exultation, the sounds of ecstasy and holiness.

*The Song of Self, the Song of Nation, the Song of Humanity, the Song of World-Creation – they all symphonize together within this person at every moment and at all times. And this perfection in its plenitude ascends to become the song of holiness, the song of El (God), the song of Israel, with passionate intensity and beauty, with fierce integrity and grandeur. Yisrael shir El – Israel [means] the song of God. It is a simple song, a twofold song, a threefold song, a fourfold song. It is the **Song of Songs** of Solomon, Shir haShirim asher liShlomo, [the song] of the King Solomon in whom is the peace of wholeness.*[96]

In this magnificent prose poem of Rabbi Kook, the ascending, expanding scope of human caring is explored. Each level is needed and valued. Yet the poet clearly teaches that, while no level of embrace is completely left behind, movement from one step to the next is urgent and natural in human development. Aiming for perfection, it is not nearly enough to embrace one's own needs or even one's own people's needs. Stretching to include the entirety of the human family with its many races, faiths, and cultures is a worthy and important goal. Yet even consciousness and concern reaching fellow human beings around the earth is insufficient for a fully developed and complete person. The highest level is to expand to every living creature,

---

96 Kook, Rabbi Avraham Yitzchok, "Shir Meruba", "The Fourfold Song" Translated from the Hebrew by Benjamin J. Samuels

animal and plant that shares the biosphere and even to worlds beyond. It is so easy to become stuck on a lower level and even to devote one's life meaningfully in pursuit of good but limited ends. While valuing each level, the vision of the poet is that even those worthy pursuits are insufficient.

Rabbi Kook's soaring spirit reaches very high. Were he alive in this era of unprecedented climate change caused by human hands, I have little doubt he would have asked for still one more step: to value and care for the platform on which every living being depends, the air, the water, and the land. Facing the onslaught of extreme weather events, perhaps he would have ventured further to declare an urgency to reach this fifth and higher level of concern. In one integrated, and tightly interdependent web of life, nothing can be omitted. No animal, no plant, neither air, nor water, nor land can be neglected. **Where an aspect of creation has no voice, the human family must endeavor to provide that voice.**

Where Responsibility Lies

Once when addressing an assembly of cantors, Abraham Joshua Heschel made this audacious statement:

It is man who is the Cantor of the universe and in whose life the secret of cosmic prayer is disclosed.[97]

We cannot know all the implications of these dramatic words, but they are very suggestive of the special role and responsibility we have for the well-being of the planet. In a synagogue setting, the ideal cantor can humbly embrace the prayers of everyone in his or her presence and offer them as an eloquent prayer before God. This role of representing a much larger whole before the Creator seems like a welcome and appropriate challenge for each member of the human family as Cantor for all of creation. Vested with consciousness and the ability to articulate our thoughts and dreams fully,

---

97 Heschel, Abraham Joshua, The Insecurity of Freedom, "The Vocation of the Cantor", (New York: Schocken Books, 1972), p. 245

enabled to imagine and take dramatic action, we can survey the state of our planet, appreciate its grandeur, assess its crises, determine their cause, and creatively work towards solutions. With our gifts of intellect and speech, we are called upon to represent every other species and even the inanimate earth itself. While we depend upon each other in the web of life on earth, every species and the inanimate partners which compose our ecosystem rely on us to see, feel, speak, and act in ways they cannot. We are the only actors that can choose to alter our behavior. We are the only sentient beings who can seek and implement solutions so urgently needed. If we harbor doubts about our capacity to make a difference in solving a global issue, we should recall the wise teaching of Rabbi Nachman of Breslav, Chassidic leader in the 19th Century:

אִם אַתָּה מַאֲמִין שֶׁיְּכוֹלִים לְקַלְקֵל, תַּאֲמִין שֶׁיְּכוֹלִין לְתַקֵּן.

If you believe that we can cause ruin, then believe that we are able to repair.[98]
There is perhaps no end to the damage that we can inflict upon this planet, but we are blessed with an equivalent ability to heal the harm we have done. **We are the spokespersons of the universe. We can speak, and we can act.**

Perhaps the best expression of the singular responsibility for human action is found in this eloquent midrash:

רְאֵה אֶת מַעֲשֵׂה הָאֱלֹהִים כִּי מִי יוּכַל לְתַקֵּן אֵת אֲשֶׁר עִוְּתוֹ, בְּשָׁעָה שֶׁבָּרָא הַקָּדוֹשׁ בָּרוּךְ הוּא אֶת אָדָם הָרִאשׁוֹן, נְטָלוֹ וְהֶחֱזִירוֹ עַל כָּל אִילָנֵי גַּן עֵדֶן, וְאָמַר לוֹ, רְאֵה מַעֲשַׂי כַּמָּה נָאִים וּמְשֻׁבָּחִין הֵן, וְכָל מַה שֶׁבָּרָאתִי בִּשְׁבִילְךָ בָּרָאתִי, תֵּן דַּעְתְּךָ שֶׁלֹּא תְקַלְקֵל וְתַחֲרִיב אֶת עוֹלָמִי, שֶׁאִם קִלְקַלְתָּ אֵין מִי שֶׁיְּתַקֵּן אַחֲרֶיךָ

Look at God's work - for who can straighten what He has twisted? (Ecclesiastes 7:13). When the Blessed Holy One created the first human, God took him and led him round all the trees of the Garden of Eden and said to him: "Look at My works, how beautiful and praiseworthy they are! And

---

98 Rabbi Nachman of Breslav, This passage is among his most notable teachings.

all that I have created, it was for you that I created it. **Pay attention that you do not corrupt and destroy My world: if you corrupt it, there is no one to repair it after you.**"[99]

---

99 Kohelet Rabba 7:13

Epilogue

From Values to Action

This brief survey of Jewish sources addressing the crisis of climate change would be an idle exercise were it not to move us to action. I could not write these words in good conscience if I were not determined to change and to seek meaningful ways to serve and to guard this Earth.

Since the founding of our modest climate action group L'olam Va-ed, its members have sought to make climate action a continual and vital part of the life of our congregation. We have sought experts who could teach us and the congregation to be more knowledgeable so that we could engage more wisely. We have found partners in our community and across the country committed to this sacred work. We joined with JTree, now a part of Adamah, to plant thousands of trees in our national forests. We assisted in a campaign of a local agency, Climate Resilient Communities (CRC), to provide relief in the form of air purifiers to less privileged neighbors whose lives are unequally impacted by climate change. We hosted an electric vehicle event at our synagogue in cooperation with the city of Palo Alto. We have initiated an effort to reduce food waste in our homes. Colossal food waste in our country exists alongside widespread hunger, and we know that food waste in city dumps results in substantial methane emissions. We've co-sponsored a Jewish Community Sustainability Fair with active members of a neighboring congregation to bring together a wide array of government agencies and NGOs to demonstrate how rich are the choices we have to make a contribution to a sustainable planet. We know we have barely begun.

Our choices are but a few of myriad ways to commit to become an upstander in this time of crisis. More resources are listed in the pages ahead. Everyone, young and older, has a vital role to play.

In Jewish tradition, when we say a blessing for a Mitzvah we are about to perform, we must not delay carrying out the action specified in the blessing.

To pronounce the words of the blessing without acting immediately would be considered a "vain blessing", a serious transgression. To me, the mandate from Torah highlighted above constitute one large, amorphous, compelling blessing. Now we must act.

Acknowledgements

I have been blessed with many partners in the composition of this book. I am very grateful to the members of L'olam Va-ed from my congregation, Kol Emeth in Palo Alto, who listened patiently to my Div're Torah at our Steering Team meetings during almost the last three years. Their attention and their responses to my presentations encouraged me to continue my quest. In a real sense, this book is a compilation of words of Torah I shared with this devoted team.

Generous readers of my manuscript asked pointed questions and reviewed my text line by line. I cannot sufficiently thank Rabbi Amy Eilberg, Marianna Grossman, Rev. Douglas Huneke, Dr. Adriane Leveen, Lorri Lewis, my wife, Dr. Sherwin Lewis, my brother, Prof. Ken Manaster, Prof. Charlotte Fonrobert, Dr. Phil Metz, Miriam Schulman, Prof. Alon Tal, and Nechama Tamler for their time and heartfelt effort. Far beyond my ask, their careful reading has shaped and focused almost every line of my book. Their granular approach and the big questions they asked led to many needed edits. I seriously want to consider my readers as my co-authors!

The cover of the book was created by Kim Howard, a gifted artist and friend. She originally drew this image for a book of stories for children which I had written, part of a series entitled *Mini Adventures in Jerusalem.* The image seemed perfect to capture the key message of this book: our responsibility to care for the Earth.

I am grateful to Rashida Basrai for designing this work as she has for so much of my previous writing. In her hands, I know that no detail will be overlooked. Her caring and her friendship sustain me.

My association with HaKodesh Press stretches back over ten years. Catalina Popoveniuc, my editor, has been a constant source of encouragement. I am very grateful for her faith in me as an author and for the efficiency with which she has guided my work to publication. Even from her office in Estonia, I know that I can depend on prompt advice and action.

My beloved wife, Lorri, sustains me every day. Like families everywhere, our fondest hope is that generations to come in which we have invested so much of our life's hopes and effort would have a healthy wondrous planet on which to live and to thrive, an awe-inspiring place where they might make their dreams come to life. I am in my ninth decade, maybe the first generation to worry about what kind of tomorrow we are bestowing on those that come after us. This book represents my humble prayer that we will awaken in time to preserve and perfect this magnificent Earth for generations yet unborn of every species under the sun.

Resources

Jewish Books Related to Climate

Benstein, Jeremy, *The Way into Judaism and the Environment,* (Vermont, Jewish Lights Publishing, 2006)

Bernstein, Ellen, *Ecology and the Jewish Spirit,* (Vermont: Jewish Lights Publishing, 2000); *The Splendor of Creation,* (Cleveland: Pilgrim Press, 2005)

Heschel, Abraham Joshua, (edited by Samuel Dresner), *I Asked For Wonder,* (New York: Crossroad, 1983)

Kahn, Andreu J. (editor), *The Sacred Earth,* (New York: Central Conference of American Rabbis, 2023)

Nebil, Yonatan & Dee, Leo, *Eco Bible,* (Jerusalem: The Interfaith Center For Sustainable Development, 2021), Volumes I & II

Tal, Alon, *Making Climate Tech Work, Policies that Drive Innovation* (Washington, Island Press, 2024)

Waskow, Arthur, *Torah of the Earth,* (Jewish Lights, 2000), Volume I

General Books on Climate

Carlson, Rachel, *Silent Spring,* (New York: Houghton Mifflin, 2002)

Gore, Al, *An Inconvenient Truth: The Crisis of Global Warming,* (New York: Viking, 2007)

Hayhoe, Katherine, *Saving Us,* (New York: One Signal Publishers, 2021)

Leopold, Aldo, *The Sand County Almanac and Other Writings on Ecology and Conservation,* (New York: The Library of America, 2013)

Lowman, Meg, *The Arbornaut,* (New York: Farrar, Straus, & Giroux, 2021)

Powers, Richard, *The Overstory,* (London:Vintage Press, 2019)

Robinson, Kim Stanley, *The Ministry for the Future,* (New York: Orbit Press, 2020)

Simard, Suzanne, *Finding the Mother Tree,* (New York: Knopf, 2021)

Wallace-Wells, David. *The Uninhabitable Earth,* (New York: Crown, 2019)

Wilson, E. O., *The Creation: An Appeal To Save Life on Earth,* (New York: W.H. Norton & Company, 2006)

Jewish Non-Profits Devoted to Healing the Climate

Adama (Adamah.org)

Coalition on the Environment and Jewish Life (www.coejl.org)

Dayenu (Dayenu.org)

Jewish Climate Action Network (Jewishclimate.org)

The Shalom Center (Theshalomcenter.org)

Faith Based Resources on Climate

Interfaith Power & Light (Interfaithpower.org)

Pope Francis & the Catholic Church, *Laudato Si': On Care for Our Common Home,* (Rome: The Vatican, 2015)

How Precious the Ground on Which We Stand:
Jewish Values That Could Save the Earth

"How Precious the Ground on Which We Stand" – That is how you'll feel about this holy Creation after you read Rabbi Lewis's rich, practical journey into Judaism's traditions and teachings on the stewardship of Creation. Reading this book inspired in me a deeper appreciation of this "precious ground" and my responsibility to continue working to preserve and protect what has been entrusted to us. Lewis's accessible rabbinic insights will be a blessing to all who care for the Creator's Creation.

– REV. DOUGLAS K. HUNEKE, Author, *The Moses of Rovno* and *The Stones Will Cry Out,* Senior Minister Emeritus. Westminster Presbyterian Church, Tiburon, CA

Our planet is on life support. These are grave times. Yet I can still find solace in the newest book by Rabbi Sheldon Lewis, HOW PRECIOUS THE GROUND ON WHICH WE STAND: JEWISH VALUES THAT COULD SAVE THE EARTH. With a clear moral vision Lewis conveys the many ways in which the Hebrew Bible celebrates the natural world as a sacred creation that we must cherish and work to preserve. His words are glorious, his vision illuminating. Reading this book fills me with joy.

– DR. ADRIANE LEVEEN, Senior Lecturer in Hebrew Bible, Hebrew Union College, New York, Co-Founder of Climate Action Network, NYC

With deep personal concern and a scholar's strength, Rabbi Lewis connects enduring Jewish wisdom with our immediate, existential responsibility to save the Earth. This concise, gently eloquent synthesis of timeless teachings enriches our understanding as it forcefully calls us to action.

– KENNETH A. MANASTER, Professor Emeritus of Environmental Law
Author, *Environmental Protection And Justice,* Santa Clara University, Santa Clara, California

What does Judaism have to say about humanity's most pressing crisis? Rabbi Shelly Lewis has written an engaging, scholarly and inspiring book about how Jewish tradition should inform our personal response to climate change: required reading for anyone who cares about the future of Creation.

– PROFESSOR ALON TAL, former chair of the Knesset subcommittee on the Environment and Climate, Tel Aviv University

When Rabbi Lewis was about to retire, his last Shabbat d'var torah was about the environment and climate change. He spoke passionately, vigorously and with great energy until he was almost shouting, definitely red in the face. After listening to our beloved Rabbi for 33 years, we knew that he only sermonized like this very rarely. This signaled that climate was a topic that needed to be seriously heeded and paid attention to. Of course, we didn't. But now, 18 years later, none of us is free to opt out. This book marries the core principles of Judaism in the Torah with the mandate to actively engage in personal behavior that will reduce global warming, and that not changing old habits means we violate Jewish tradition and commandments at our peril.

– NECHAMA TAMLER, Jewish Educator and Climate Activist, Founder of "L'olam Va-ed", Climate action team at Congregation Kol Emeth, Palo Alto, CA.